Religion *and the* Rise *of*
Modern Culture

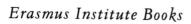

Erasmus Institute Books

Religion *and the* Rise *of* Modern Culture

LOUIS DUPRÉ

University of Notre Dame Press
Notre Dame, Indiana

Designed by Wendy McMillen
Set in 11.8/14 Pavane by EM Studio, Inc.

Library of Congress Cataloging-in-Publication Data

Dupré, Louis K., 1925–
Religion and the rise of modern culture / Louis Dupre.
p.   cm. — (Erasmus Institute books)
Includes index.
ISBN-13: 978-0-268-02594-6 (pbk. : alk. paper)
ISBN-10: 0-268-02594-0 (pbk. : alk. paper)
1. Christianity and culture—Europe—History.   2. Europe—Intellectual life.
3. Christianity and culture—Germany—History.   4. Germany—Intellectual life.
5. Church history—Modern period, 1500–   I. Title.
BR735.D86   2008
261.0943—dc22

2007051040

contents

preface

The following pages contain the text of the Erasmus Lectures, delivered at the University of Notre Dame during the academic year 2005–2006. For me the meaning of the occasion was enhanced by its occurring at an institute that bears the name of the father of Europe's spiritual unity, a teacher at my alma mater. Erasmus taught tolerance at a time of intolerance and remains a guide in the religious turmoil of the present.

Writing down a previously spoken text proved to be a sobering experience. The expectant faces, probing questions, intellectual challenges, which had made the delivery so exciting, no longer sustained the writing. To compensate for their absence, I have attempted to preserve at least some of the spontaneity of the original setting. Still, as lectures turned into chapters, theses proclaimed with the presumed authority of an invited speaker often assumed a tentative quality. Questions never asked or never answered glaringly appeared through the assertiveness of the spoken words. I became painfully aware of the provisional character of the ideas expressed, especially in the second part of the lectures. I hope to cast them in a more definitive form during the next years. As the lectures appear here, they nevertheless recapture for me the stimulating dialogue with an intelligent and generous audience engaged in a common search for the nature of modern culture.

They also revived the gratitude I continue to feel toward my wonderful hosts, Robert Sullivan and Dianne Phillips, the director and associate director of the Erasmus Institute, as well as the joy of reliving the presence of friends long out of sight yet marvelously unchanged, Cyril O'Reagan and Kathy Kaveney. I gratefully recall making the acquaintance of men and women with whom I felt an instant spiritual affinity, especially Dean Mark Roche, Professor Fred Dallmayer, and poet Henry Weinfield. To all of them I dedicate this memoir of a shared experience.

Special thanks to Barbara Hanrahan, the director of the Notre Dame Press, and to Rebecca DeBoer, its managing editor, for their gracious kindness and patience.

The first three chapters recapitulate much that I have developed in *Passage to Modernity* (Yale University Press, 1993) and *The Enlightenment and the Intellectual Development of Modern Culture* (Yale University Press, 2004). Parts of chapter 4 have been published in "On the Intellectual Sources of Modern Atheism," *International Journal for Philosophy of Religion* 45 (1999): 1–11.

Introduction

Religion and the Rise of Modern Culture

The title of this book might raise questions. Does man's participation in the eternal ever change? Interpretations, rituals, even moral precepts become transformed over the centuries. Yet does the religious attitude not remain constant within the flux of time? It does, indeed. But the individual and social response to religion also includes the task of integrating that attitude within the warp and woof of existence in a particular culture at a particular time. The manner in which the devout fulfill that task differs from one period to another. Its nature is at least in part determined by the social and intellectual conditions prevailing at the time of the response.

In the history of Christianity, cultural transformations may have been more substantial during the modern period than in any preceding one. The seeds of change were planted much earlier, some at the height of the Middle Ages, some even before. I shall trace them in the first two chapters. For over a millennium Western culture had been the culture of Christianity. At the beginning of the modern age, culture and religion assumed a certain independence vis-à-vis each other. During the Enlightenment, separation turned into opposition.

Later their relation became more conciliatory. Yet the Church never regained its former authority over society. Theology, once the dominant science that had integrated all others, definitively lost its commanding position.

In the first part of these lectures (ch. 1–4) I shall sketch the gradual weakening of the Christian synthesis, partly as a result of the breakdown of the form principle (ch. 1) and partly because of an ever-growing distinction between the orders of nature and of grace (ch. 2). In addition to these changes and partly because of them, modern culture increasingly came to regard the human subject as the sole source of meaning and value. Combined, these factors gradually severed Christianity from the culture it had built. The Enlightenment marked a turning point in this process of secularization (ch. 3). Atheism became, for the first time, a real threat to religion (ch. 4).

After the French Revolution and mostly as a reaction against it, religion, but not necessarily Christian faith, once again appeared destined to play a significant role in intellectual life. Yet now the roles were reversed. Rather than dominating them, religion became transformed by intellectual and moral principles conceived independently of faith and often against it. In the second part of these lectures I shall investigate the new situation in three areas. First is in the literature of Romanticism. To illustrate this I have selected three poets whose work profoundly affected religious attitudes of the contemporary age: Goethe, Schiller, and Hölderlin (ch. 5). Second, the related impact of idealist philosophy significantly contributed toward reunifying religion with the entire life of the mind. No one illustrates this better than Schelling, who incorporated mythology and revelation as essential parts within his philosophical system (ch. 6). Third, theology itself underwent a basic transformation during this period, as the early Romantic Schleiermacher and the late Romantic Kierkegaard prove (ch. 7).

I have deliberately limited the discussion to German sources, because in Germany the Enlightenment had achieved its influence mainly within and through theology. German poets, philosophers, and theologians consciously attempted to achieve a new synthesis of religion and culture. Moreover, during this critical period the originality of German philosophers and theologians surpassed that of their contemporaries in France and England. I conclude with some general reflections about the impact of modernity on the contemporary state of religion and culture.

Obviously, this work presents no more than a limited perspective on the very complex relation between religion and modern culture. But I remain convinced that the basic patterns formed in the modern age, especially at the dawn of the contemporary era, have maintained themselves. The chapters here presented are to be considered *capita selecta* of a more comprehensive project. The reader is encouraged to read them as such.

chapter O N E

The Form of Modernity

Until recent years some cultural historians restricted the concept of modern culture to the Enlightenment. They assumed that the main significance of fifteenth-century humanism, of the Renaissance, and even of the first part of the classical seventeenth century consisted in preparing the mental attitudes of the Enlightenment. Jacob Burckhardt's *Civilization of the Renaissance in Italy* may serve as a model of this approach. But principles such as the equation of the real with the objective, the emancipation from past political and religious traditions, or the autonomy of reason, characteristic of Enlightenment thought, by no means define the early modern epoch. Even today, the assumption of a straight continuity between the phases of modernity has not entirely vanished. To be sure, there is a modern culture, a mode of thinking, feeling, and creating that stretches from the fifteenth through the twentieth century. But it arrived in successive waves, each one bringing its own principles, which, though continuous with those of the previous one, do not follow from them with logical necessity. Modernity is an ongoing creative process that even today has not reached completion.

By the end of the fourteenth century the cloud of dark resignation that hung over a civilization half destroyed by the plague and an
intellectual life lost in a moribund theology began to lift. In those
southern regions of Europe, which had never fully broken with ancient culture, the old sense of dignity was revived and the rediscovery
of the past inspired a new confidence in the future. Nature suddenly
assumed a more humane appearance: it once again was thought to reflect human emotions, and appeared eminently worthy of human ex-
ploration.

Classical and Medieval Precedents

What, then, was the past out of which, and eventually in contrast
to which, modernity developed? In the first place there was the classical culture, which had never ceased to influence the medieval one,
and which suddenly in fifteenth-century Italy intensified that influence. Particularly, the concept of *form* acquired a new significance.
For the Greeks, it had been both a physical quality and an intellectual
principle. Proportion was a quality of nature as well as a primary
attribute of the gods, who, by their formal perfection, surpassed the
perishable, imperfect humans. In Plato's thought, the notion of form
implied the profound metaphysical principle that it belongs to the nature of the real to *appear* and to do so in an orderly, intelligible way.
For a long time the Greeks had succeeded in preserving the
unique identity of their culture, despite its dispersion over such remote islands as Sicily and such distant regions as Asia Minor and
Southern Italy. It continued to do so for a while even after the Hellenistic empires extended it to the entire Middle East. At the end of
that period Greek culture confronted its supreme challenge. It began
when, in the Septuagint translation, Jews opened their sacred books
to the Gentile *oekumene*. In Alexandria, now the intellectual capital
of the Greek world, where this event had occurred, the Jewish philosopher Philo attempted to reconcile Jerusalem with Athens. But the
Greek mind felt a strong aversion to the idea of a God who no longer
formed a part of the cosmos but was its transcendent Creator. That
early Christians, steeped in Jewish theology, fared no better in the

eyes of the Greeks appeared in the poor reception Paul's speech received on the Areopagus (Acts 17:32–34).

Christians did not give up the attempt to reconcile their faith with Hellenic wisdom. Religiously oriented Neoplatonic thought provided a fertile ground for dialogue. The Cappadocian Fathers adopted much of Plotinus's philosophy, and soon most of the Christian East followed. For the last of the great classical thinkers, the divine still dwelled *within* the cosmos, yet at the same time transcended it. This truce between Christian and ancient culture was not to last.

The tension between the two worldviews appeared when some of the eighth-century Macedonian emperors of Byzantium, who considered the iconic representations of Christ and the saints to conflict with the idea of a God hidden in impenetrable light, banned them from the churches. Most Christians resisted, appealing to the mystery of the Incarnation, which had forged an indissoluble link between God and human nature in the person of Christ. They prevailed. But the impact of the same mystery of the Incarnation, which had supported the return of orthodoxy in the East, eventually was to cause the breakup of the Hellenic-Christian synthesis in the Latin West.

The problem arose in the wake of what was perhaps the most attractive development of medieval Christianity: Francis of Assisi and his thirteenth-century followers extended the effect of the Incarnation to the entire created world. Even the image of Jesus changed. He was not merely God's eternal Word among us, but a concrete human being. Francis concluded that Christ's human nature itself deserved to be honored and adored. The religious humanism he had initiated blossomed into an artistic movement in which, contrary to the Greek primacy of the universal, the highest spiritual meaning resided in the individual. It was the time of the great innovators in painting, Cimabue, Duccio, and Giotto, and in poetry, Dante, Petrarch, and Boccaccio. Soon it became apparent how much this new idea of individual form conflicted with the classical one adopted by earlier Christian culture, in which only the universal had intellectual birthright.

Against the background of this new vision, the Franciscan John Duns Scotus accomplished an intellectual revolution. The *doctor subtilis* understood that the Greek notion of form was inadequate for expressing the mystery of Christ: it omitted what Christians of his time had come to see as most essential, namely, the individuality of the person of Christ. So he added to the ancient hierarchy of forms a *forma individualis* to legitimate the unique *thisness* of the historical Jesus. His move was not totally unprecedented. Plotinus himself (in *Enneads* 4, 3, 7) had written that souls are formally individuated before becoming united to the body. Even Aquinas, concerned to preserve the spiritual integrity of the soul after death, had declared it to be unaffected by its physical embodiment (*Summa Theologiae* I, q.7, a.2, and I, q.50, a.2). Nonetheless, reluctant to abandon the Greek principle of universality altogether, he had qualified his position by claiming that the human soul, though spiritual, attains individuality through its relation to matter—the mysterious *materia quantitate signata.* Scotus went further. For him, individuality itself was a form, the ultimate one in the Platonic hierarchy.

The *Via Moderna* and the New Humanist Form

Another Franciscan, William of Ockham, brought this development to its conclusion when he denied that universals—including all ancient *forms*—in any way exist. Everything in nature as well as in the mind is singular. That a substance bears a certain resemblance to another is a matter of subjective perception, not the effect of their sharing a common nature. Ockham thereby totally abandoned the assumption, deeply entrenched in Platonic thinking, that universal forms exist in reality as well as in ideas. He admitted the need for universal concepts and for names with a universal significance, but asserted that universals existed neither *beyond* (Plato) nor *inside* reality (Aristotle). They are mere constructions of the mind. Ockham's critique of form obviously spelled the end of the Greek cosmotheological synthesis. One might also assume it to be the end of medieval philosophy. Yet the notion of form, both the classical and the Christian, was to acquire new life in the humanist movement.

The rise of Italian humanism coincided with that of the nominalist *via moderna* in philosophy. At the surface the two movements appear unrelated. Humanism unquestioningly accepted the form principle as articulated by Plato and his followers. Indeed, the movement itself was first and foremost a new search for form through language.[1] Having started as a rhetorical movement, humanism aimed at studying the Latin writers and at imitating their style, not only in the ancient language but also in the vernacular. Humanists attempted to revive the formal perfection of classical authors and generally objected to the late medieval language of Scholasticism. Nonetheless, as Paul Kristeller has shown, humanism preserved a strong link with the rhetorical tradition of the Middle Ages. Most humanists remained loyal to the medieval worldview and, indeed, to much of its philosophy.

Nominalist philosophy, though it undermined the ancient notion of universal form, agreed with humanism on at least one crucial issue: the supreme significance of language. It thereby added substantial weight to the rhetorical exercises of the humanists and, in fact, contributed to their raising the practice of language into a pursuit of ideal form. According to Lorenzo Valla, the last and most articulate of the early humanists, the nominalist conception of language reduces philosophical concepts to their concrete, earthly origins and thereby establishes a new, more direct link between thought and reality. He regarded nominalist philosophy as needlessly complicated, however, and he had no use for the nominalism of the Scholastics. His theory may rightly be called a "humanist counter-nominalism" (Charles Trinkaus).

The humanist movement characteristically stressed poetic and artistic creativity. In one of his prose writings Dante defined the attitude that was to become typical of modern culture as one of unlimited confidence in man's creative power. Even as God created all forms *ex nihilo,* so the poet in inventing metaphorical meaning creates a poetic form that did not exist before. Dante and most early humanists regarded this creative power as a gift of God. The artists and poets of the Renaissance increasingly attributed it to human genius. All agreed on the ancient rule that art must be an imitation of nature. They regarded nature itself as a work of art, though an impure one

---

1. Johan Huizinga, *The Waning of the Middle Ages* (*Herfsttij der Middeleeuwen,* 1924) (Garden City, N.Y.: Doubleday, 1956), pp. 323–35.

that the artist must bring to formal perfection. The two currents, on one side early humanism and the Renaissance, on the other the philosophical *via moderna,* initiated modern culture.

Galileo's thought presents the transition to the second modern period. He drew from both sources of the early modern age. Confident, creative, artistically gifted, and deeply religious, he initially had much in common with some of the Italian humanists. In his early writings he refers to the divine wisdom as *inherent in nature,* causing it to follow ideal laws of simplicity and regularity. Observation alone, however, does not suffice to know a phenomenon: it must be broken down into ideal elements. In his later work Galileo abandoned much of this Platonic idealism and avoided constraining the complexity of nature within the demands of philosophical ideals. Consequently he attempted to capture the mathematical nature of motion as actually observed rather than as ideally projected. Moreover, observation taught him that in the celestial sphere the same physical laws are valid as the ones on earth. Hence, the laws of mechanics rule the entire universe, not only the sublunary sphere, as ancient and many medieval philosophers thought.

The Loss of Form in Post-Cartesian Thought

Galileo had continued to assume that truth is inherent in the nature of reality. In this respect he differed from the position Descartes and most thinkers of the later seventeenth and the eighteenth centuries were to embrace, namely, that truth is achieved by the mind. To produce truth, the mind must first transform nature into a representation. Instead of participating in nature's immanent truth, the mind has to perform a *reconstruction* of it. Descartes intended to establish knowledge on the unshakable foundation of the mind's own laws and thus stop the flood of skepticism unleashed by nominalist theology. According to this theology, divine omnipotence was not bound by the restrictions of human reason. A lingering nominalism continued to affect Descartes' own philosophy, however, as when he attributes the intuitive insight that $2+2=4$ to a divine decree.

Doubts about the efficacy of Descartes' a priori method in science sprang up soon after he formulated it. Could nature's course be described exhaustively or even functionally in mathematical terms? Contrary to Descartes' assumptions, Newton famously declared "Hypotheses non fingo." He did in fact construe hypotheses, but avoided doing so independently of observation. Yet the most serious questions about the applicability of Descartes' mathematical approach came from the budding life sciences. Buffon unsuccessfully tried to apply the mechanistic method to the study of animal life and was forced to abandon the effort.

In modern cosmology the notion of substance came to replace that of form without major consequences. But because of the complex relation between mind and body, that notion proved inadequate for defining personal identity. Yet Descartes had no other option, if he was to include all beings within a simple comprehensive world system. To maintain the spiritual quality of the mind, he had to separate it from the body as an independent "substance." In his bodily substance the person shares a mechanistic world common to all material things. Though man surpasses the laws of mechanics, yet through his body he indirectly forms a part of the world system. If the body constituted a reality in its own right, it had to be called a substance as well as the mind. Aristotelian and Scholastic philosophy had escaped this dualism of body and soul. For both, the soul was the *form* of the body, while still retaining a certain independence of it. Aristotle spoke of the double function of one soul. Aquinas called the soul *forma substantialis subsistens,* a term that embraced both functions.

How much the replacement of form by substance militated against the traditional position and indeed against Descartes' own fundamental insight appeared soon after his death. Materialists such as La Mettrie and Helvétius argued that he had accepted half the materialist theory. Had he not declared that the entire animal world formed part of a single material universe and was subject to mechanical laws? Why, then, had he inconsistently made an exception for the mind? No *essential* difference separates human knowledge from animal cognition. Condillac in his *Treatise on Sensations* had shown that one as well as the other is derived from sensations caused by physiological processes. Baron d'Holbach, the unanointed leader of the French materialists, confidently concluded: "Man is a physical being." This, of course, marked the end of the form principle. Only one homogeneously material nature remained.

A comparable change occurred in Britain. Locke, despite his firm opposition to materialism, nevertheless decided that the mind ought to be studied by the same method that was yielding such remarkable results in the natural sciences. Rather than accepting a formal principle of psychic unity, he chose to break experience down into the simple units of sensations and reflections. This elementarist reduction caused major problems for maintaining the traditional unity of the self and even more for treating it as a single substance. Nonetheless Locke continued to accept a common belief in the presence of a single substratum to the multiplicity of sensations and reflections. The fact that the data of consciousness appear in clusters and in a relative continuity induces the mind to *assume* the existence of such a substratum. We believe it to be a spiritual substance. But must consciousness be the exclusive attribute of spirit? Locke had to admit that he could not prove it.

Hume brought this argument to a more consistent conclusion. Since impressions (the atomic units in his analysis) are qualitatively distinct, they must be considered separately, and whatever can be considered separately may exist separately. There is no need for assuming a common substratum or even an intrinsic link among singular perceptions. "Self or person is not any one impression, but that to which our several impressions and ideas are supposed to have reference. . . . Pain and pleasure, grief and joy, passions and sensations succeed each other, and never all exist at the same time. It cannot, therefore, be from any of these impressions or from any other, that the idea of self is derived; and consequently there is no such idea."[2]

British empiricism eventually led to the destruction of the form principle, as sensationalism did in France. Yet French sensationalists based their empiricism upon a materialist presupposition, namely, that sensations and impressions originated as a direct effect of the impact of the physical world. Expressed in d'Holbach's crudely reductionist language: "[The person's] visible actions as well as the invisible motion interiorly excited by his will and his thoughts, are

---

2. *Treatise of Human Nature* (Oxford: Oxford University Press, 1928), Bk I, 251–52.

equally the natural effects, the necessary consequences, of his peculiar mechanism, and the impulse he received from those beings by whom he is surrounded."[3]

While rationalists and empiricists were undermining the form principle, Leibniz on the rationalist side and Shaftesbury on the empiricist one attempted to revive it. Leibniz did so by reinterpreting Newton's concept of force in the sense of an Aristotelian form, thereby enabling it to serve as a dynamic principle of the physical world and as a spiritual principle of the ideal world. For him, the soul was not a "substance" in the Cartesian sense of the term, but a monad, that is, a center of power capable of directing the subordinate monads of the body. Leibniz thereby avoided the fatal dilemma: either the person would consist of two substances, or of one material substance, which would jeopardize the spiritual nature of the mind.

Shaftesbury, inspired by Plato's idea of form, intrinsically transformed the very nature of the empiricist philosophy in which Locke had tutored him. He rejected Locke's elementarism, but accepted that philosophy should have its ground in experience. Beyond the singular experiences of particular sensations and impressions, he argued, we have the continuous experience of a persistent feeling that accompanies all stages of consciousness and links them together. That feeling of self-awareness secures the smooth transition from one perception to the next and encompasses the whole person, body and mind. Self-consciousness consists not primarily in the awareness of successive, vanishing impressions, but in the awareness of a deeper, continuous undercurrent of feeling.

In shifting the weight of selfhood to the side of feelings, Shaftesbury restored at least some of the qualities of the self as a *formative* principle. His influence proved to be enormous, in France as well as in Britain. The new significance he granted to feelings inspired a number of autobiographical writings. Their authors attempted to convey a formal unity to the self, by showing the continuity of its feelings. Rousseau in his *Confessions* identifies the self with the

---

3. Paul Henry Thiry, baron d'Holbach, *Le système de la nature* (1770) (1868; reprint, New York: Burt Franklin, 1970), p. 11.

history of his feelings. In fact, however, he does more than reproduce feelings: he produces new ones on the basis of old memories and thereby recreates the scattered experiences of the past into a unified, orderly totality. It is through a constant reconstruction of our feelings, then, that we link the past to the present and convey a real identity to life.

In chapter 5 we shall see how the great German thinkers of the late eighteenth and early nineteenth centuries, Kant, Herder, Fichte, and Schelling, replaced the static notion of substance by the dynamic one of freedom. The term *Bildung,* which expressed this ideal of self-making, came to dominate theories and programs of education. Humans ought to conform themselves to an ideal form of *humanitas.* One might regard this as at least a partial restoration of the ancient idea of form.

The Modern Idea of Truth and Transcendence

Rationalism differs from the primacy of reason, which our culture since its beginning in Greek Antiquity has considered its most prominent characteristic. The question is: Could Western rationality have avoided developing into rationalism? When Descartes identified truth with certainty, he essentially eliminated what had supported the intentional quality of knowledge, which in one way or another his predecessors in philosophy had preserved. For Plato, intelligible *forms* had constituted the core of the *real.* Truth originates neither in sense evidence nor in self-awareness, but in the contemplation of the forms. In his *Phaedo* Plato declares the soul to be "like" the forms within which it participates in knowledge, but he never identifies the two. In the *Cratylus* he insists that true learning can come only from things in themselves, that is, from the forms. Aristotle rejected the theory of independent forms, but for him also, the mind attains truth only by an intentional relation to reality. The Scholastics, despite major differences among themselves, defended an intentional theory of knowledge. All presupposed an ontological *givenness* of the real in the act of knowing.

The principles of modern thought implicitly conflicted with this assumption. That truth was to be established exclusively on the basis of the mind's own criteria of certainty directly affected the conception of transcendence. Thus, there was a sudden explosion of arguments to prove the necessary existence of what the new concept of rationality no longer needed. Not surprisingly, those arguments failed to be persuasive. Only the ontological argument, which in fact expressed the ancient belief that all thinking rested on a transcendent basis, regained new power.

Still, few thinkers embraced the "modern position" without serious reservations. Descartes himself preserved much of Augustine's doctrine, according to which the process of truth presupposes a divine illumination. In the *Third Meditation,* he actually resumes the Augustinian doctrine of the interior Master who *gives* the idea of the infinite to human consciousness. His much-criticized "ontological argument" in the *Fifth Meditation* merely explicates an idea not construed by the mind but *given* to the mind. "While from the fact that I cannot conceive God without existence, it follows that existence is inseparable from Him, and hence that the reality exists, not that my thought can bring this to pass, or impose any necessity which lies in the thing itself, i.e. the necessity of the existence of God determines me to think this way."[4] Even the famous "cogito, ergo sum" goes back to Augustine, who had written: "Si enim fallor, sum. Nam qui non est, utique nec falli potest: ac per hoc sum si fallor" (*De civitate dei,* XI, 26) (Even if I am deceived, I am; for who is not cannot be deceived, hence I am if I were deceived).

What, then, were the effects on religion of Descartes' intellectual revolution? Rationality, which formerly had constituted the essence of the real, now became the exclusive attribute of the mind. The notion of transcendence lost much of its meaning when the mind itself had to define what, by its own description, totally surpassed it. The turn to the self as the new source of meaning affected even the self's own content. Being the *subject* of meaning, the self was in fact reduced to a mere *function* that possessed no content of its own. Kant put his finger on the problem: the source of knowledge cannot become an object of knowledge.

---

4. *The Philosophical Works of Descartes,* trans. Elizabeth S. Haldane and G. R. T. Ross (Cambridge: Cambridge University Press, 1911; reprint, 1970), vol. 1, p. 181.

Did the newly defined *reason* do for the modern mind what the idea of the *cosmos* did for Greek Antiquity, or the idea of God for medieval culture? I think not, because reason had become a purely critical concept, formal and abstract, void of content. In the *Phenomenology of Spirit* Hegel describes the Enlightenment as a dialectical struggle between reason and faith, whereby faith preserved the ideal content but lost the power to justify itself, and reason retained only the critical force without the content. Critical reason imposed an abstract pattern of order on nature and society. In the French Revolution it initiated a global project to improve the entire human species.

The rationalist rhetoric strikes us today as absurdly presumptuous. Yet rationalism and its irrational counterpart were still very much alive in the twentieth century when communist ideologies attempted to impose a rationalist pattern of abstract equality upon society and when, on the opposite side, an irrational nationalism proclaimed the superiority of nation and race over all values. Who would dare to say that today the desire for rationalist engineering under yet a different banner, such as the worldwide spreading of democracy upon reluctant nations, has vanished? Or that the destructive powers of irrational racism and intolerance have finally yielded to reason?

chapter T W O

Nature and Grace

During the first two centuries Christians appear to have experienced no particular problem in integrating the idea of salvation with the vague notions of nature, mostly of Stoic origin, which were current in Rome at the time. Early Christians distanced themselves from the surrounding culture, but not so much from the idea of human nature that supported it. Even when, in the third century, Origen modeled his theory of the soul as image of the divine Word after the Platonic idea of the soul as reflecting the Nous, or when the fourth-century theologians Gregory of Nyssa and Gregory of Nazianze began to use Plotinus's concept of the divine immanence in nature for expressing God's presence in grace, no particular problems occurred. We cannot but marvel at the seamless continuity that, for centuries, integrated the mystery of grace with those constructions of Greek philosophy.

At some point during the thirteenth century the first signs appear of a growing opposition between ancient philosophy and Christian theology. The recently rediscovered works of Aristotle confronted

Latin theologians with a dilemma. Could the concept of nature, especially of human nature, as presented in these writings, be integrated with a Christian theology of grace? The so-called Averrhoist Aristotelians responded that philosophy and theology could exist independent of each other. Their theory of "double truth" was condemned, and would not reemerge before the Renaissance. Meanwhile the great Dominicans Albert and Thomas began to look for a new synthesis.

The Thomist Synthesis

Albert and Thomas understood that for such a synthesis to be possible the key Aristotelian concepts had to be subordinated to an overall Christian vision. They had to be adjusted but could be preserved. This decision, of course, had major importance in the area of ethics, on which Christians had long developed their own ideas. Thomas Aquinas marvelously succeeded in integrating the Aristotelian theory of virtue within a Christian framework. He conceived of these natural virtues as preparing the theological ones of faith, hope, and charity, and he carefully circumnavigated the cliffs that might threaten such a reconstruction. Aristotle's idea of nature implied a teleology, which would naturally resist any subordination to a higher end. For Thomas also, virtue, good citizenship, and the theoretical life counted as final ends, but in addition to the attainment of natural human perfection, they played a necessary yet instrumental role in the process leading to the person's supernatural destination.

But could Aristotelian nature submit to being so directed toward an end that surpassed its capacities as well as its aspirations? That question could be answered affirmatively only if nature itself contained a "natural desire" for God. Aquinas unambiguously advanced the thesis that indeed the *possibility* of such a desire existed. But did he also recognize its reality? In the *Summa contra Gentiles* III, 25, he treats the theme from two different yet related points of view. First, he posits that each being seeks to realize the full potential of its nature. Truth and goodness are perfections, which a spiritual being naturally desires, although the limited capacity of a finite being prevents it from ever fully attaining them. The desire (*appetitus*), then, would be natural, even though its full realization lies beyond the potential of human nature.

Next, he claims that all creatures seek a kind of similitude with the Creator in accordance with their nature. For intellectual creatures, such a natural ideal would consist in acquiring the highest knowledge. That, according to Thomas, means knowing what God knows, namely, God's own Being. An intellectual dynamism, then, moves human knowledge toward a knowledge of God: "Intelligere deum est finis omnis intellectualis substantiae" (*Summa contra Gentiles* III, 5; cf. also III, 52). In his analysis of St. Thomas's position, Georges Cottier writes: "The natural desire has its source in the metaphysical nature of the intellect. Its object is *Being* in its full extent, even though a knowledge that attains the first Being only through inferior analogates may fall short of this ideal. But by nature it spontaneously moves toward the perfect knowledge of its object."[1] This very desire propels thinking and knowing to pursue, beyond each limited good or object of knowledge, an unlimited one. Thomas assumes that a natural desire cannot be idle, even though the human mind is incapable of satisfying it by its natural powers.

The mind cannot *demand* the satisfaction of a desire whose fulfillment lies entirely beyond its capacity. The desire for God, then, may be called "natural" only to the extent that it seeks its fulfillment in general, not in a theologically specific way. As long as the link with a transcendent reality was conceived as inherent in the person's spiritual nature, the religious experience (especially the mystical) anticipated the fulfillment and, at least in part, satisfied the natural desire for God. For Thomas, as well as for Bonaventure and Scotus, philosophy itself, the natural knowledge of *Being*, had a mystical quality: the desire for knowledge was driven by a divine dynamism.

However one interprets Thomas's position, he decisively discarded the idea of a "supernatural" order of reality which would be simply juxtaposed to the natural one. For him, the term "supernatural" refers to the *means*, which enable nature to attain its one ultimate

---

1. P. Georges Cottier, "Désir naturel de voir Dieu," *Gregorianum* 78 (1997): 679–98, esp. 695–96.

end, not to a different *order of reality*. Thus in the *Summa contra Gentiles* he writes: "In order that man may be brought to his ultimate end by his own operations, a form must be superadded to him from which his operations may get a certain efficacy in meriting his ultimate end."[2] Also: "But to man, in order that he may attain his ultimate end, there is added a perfection higher than his own nature, namely grace."[3] Nor does Thomas ever use the expression "pure nature" to refer to nature independent of divine grace. The concept of nature as an independent reality originated in the wake of later, nominalist theologies. Neither he nor any theologian before the sixteenth century distinguishes an "order of grace" separate from, and superimposed on, the "order" of grace. There is only *one order* that includes both nature and grace, and one ultimate end.

Two theses, however, threatened the balance of this synthesis. In contrast to Scotus, who was to interpret the Incarnation as an essential moment in God's self-communication, Thomas considered the Incarnation a divine response to the fall. The fall had distorted nature to a point where it had assumed some kind of false independence. He thereby weakened his position that grace is merely a supernatural means enabling the person to attain his "natural end."

Secondly, he contends that the relation between God and creation must be conceived as a causal one. In his early works, in which the Neoplatonic influence was still very strong, Thomas had conceived of this relation as consisting primarily in a participation in the divine Being. In the later *Summa Theologiae,* however, he adopted the causal explanation stating that the act of existing is the effect of a transcendent Cause, whereby creating means "to produce the existence of things" (*Summa Theologiae* I, q.45, a.6). But if God, defined as pure Being, in the creative act "produces" finite being, God is separated from creation, as an efficient cause is from its effect. The concept of causality in Thomas has not yet been reduced to mere efficient

---

2. *Summa contra gentes,* III, ch. 150, trans. Vernon J. Bourke (New York: Doubleday, 1956).

3. Ibid., ch. 152. Both texts of Thomas are quoted by Henri de Lubac in *Surnaturel* (Paris: Aubier, 1946).

causality, as it was to be in most modern philosophy. It even appears to have included some idea of participation. At the beginning of the *Summa* he writes: "Being is innermost in each thing and most fundamentally present within all things, since it is formal in respect of everything found in a thing. . . . Hence it must be that God is in all things, and innermostly" (*Summa Theologiae* I, q.8, a.1). Yet in the reply to the first objection against this position he stipulates *how* God is present and writes: "He is in all things as *cause* of the being of all things." This was a perfectly reasonable answer, but in the context of the *later* understanding of causality as efficient causality, it could easily be misunderstood to mean: God produces all things as a cause produces an effect.

Despite the tension caused by Thomas's medicinal interpretation of redemption and the emphasis on efficient causality, the Thomist concept of nature still continues to receive its definitive interpretation from the order of grace. To be sure, as a follower of Aristotle, St. Thomas also uses a purely philosophical concept of nature. But this object of rational reflection, independently of grace, is an abstraction, or as Karl Rahner called it, a residual concept (*ein Restbegriff*)[4] that must be understood through its dialectical counterpart. It has nothing in common with the *natura pura* which sixteenth-century theologians presented as an independent reality. In the real order, nature must be conceived within the perspective of grace, but in comparing it with pre-Christian philosophy, Thomas does not take into account what revelation teaches about grace. We must conclude, then, that nature in the Thomistic synthesis possesses a transcendent openness to grace and a *desiderium naturale* toward a fulfillment in grace.

The Thomist synthesis continued to inspire poets and artists. Dante's majestic combination of nature and grace, of cosmology and theology, and of politics and philosophy in *De Monarchia* and in the *Commedia* shows the creative and enduring power of St. Thomas's Christian Aristotelianism. The weakness of the synthesis consisted

---

4. Karl Rahner, *Theological Investigations,* vol. 1 (London: Barton, Longman, Todd, 1968), p. 302.

in what also was its strength, namely, its complexity. This complexity made it liable, at the slightest imbalance, to harden into a dualism of a base and a superstructure. This is, of course, what happened once the distinction between nature and the supernatural became interpreted as one between two separate orders, as Siger of Brabant or Boethius of Dacia did. They unraveled the synthesis of Christian revelation with Aristotelian philosophy until it was no more than a juxtaposition of two orders of being. Thomas successfully fought them. But the fact that a combination of theology with Aristotelian philosophy had led to those excesses raised questions about the soundness of Thomas's own synthesis. In 1277 Etienne Tempier, the archbishop of Paris, condemned some of his theses.

Nominalism, Reformation, Humanism

Aristotle's philosophy was in fact neither the immediate nor the primary cause of the separation of grace and nature in the modern age. The movement most responsible for the separation was the very one that had inspired the resistance against Aristotelianism, namely, nominalism. Nominalist theologies destroyed the intelligibility of the relation between Creator and creature. If creation depends on the inscrutable decision of a God who totally surpasses the laws of human reason, nature loses its intrinsic intelligibility. Grace also becomes a blind result of a divine decree, randomly dispensed to an unprepared human nature. The emphasis upon a divine omnipotence unrestricted by rationality results in a "supernatural order" separated from nature's immanent rationality.

My intention in writing this is not to deny the benefits the nominalist way of thinking brought to the development of science. All too readily, medieval philosophy had predicted a priori the course of nature on the basis of assumed divine attributes. We remember the difficulties Galileo experienced in convincing the Aristotelians of the value of his experiments. Henceforth philosophers could no longer rely on what *had* to be the nature of a physical process, according to their idea of God's eternal reason. They were forced to find out how things actually *were* by empirical investigation. By the same token, however, the delicate medieval balance between philosophy and theology was permanently disturbed.

We may well regard religious thought of the early modern period—from the fifteenth through the seventeenth centuries—as a prolonged attempt to recover the lost unity. This took different forms. The Reformation marked a return to the earlier, pre-"Aristotelian" Christian synthesis with, however, a hazardous acceptance of the late Augustine's concept of a thoroughly corrupted nature. The humanist movement, driven by a new confidence in nature, went in the opposite direction: Christian Platonism inspired a new naturalism. By the time of the Renaissance, however, this naturalism had ceased to be Christian. Both the Reformation and the humanist movement failed in their attempt to reintegrate the natural with the supernatural. Reformed theology, aware of man's *total* involvement in the drama of sin and redemption, rejected the dual order of late medieval theology. The fall had affected human nature as well as its supernatural sanctification. Yet soon the kind of nominalist thinking whose philosophical consequences the Protestant theologians had fled infiltrated their own thought. The very seriousness with which they stressed the impact of sin—the *corruptio totalis*—led to a concept of fallen nature, which grace itself would not be able to transform intrinsically. God's "imputed" righteousness, though expressing a change in the divine attitude, left nature right where it found it. Thus a separation not unlike the earlier one between nature and a supernatural order emerged at a later stage.[5]

Indeed, the Anglican divine William Law attributed much of the secularism of the eighteenth century to the extrinsic character of a forensic theory of justification. In a few memorable pages of *The Spirit of Love* he outright rejects the notion of an "imputed" righteousness as well as the distinction between a natural and a supernatural order. Divine righteousness intrinsically transforms human nature. With Luther he is willing to call it *God's* righteousness, since it had been

---

5. In my *Passage to Modernity* I have indicated how much this judgment is to be qualified in the case of Luther and, I suspect, also of Calvin. Here I discuss only principles present in "Lutheranism" and "Calvinism."

first *received* at creation and was subsequently *restored* by divine redemption. But we ought to remember that God "calls us to own the power, presence, and operation of God in all that we feel and find in our own inward state."[6] To the extent that it intrinsically affects man's nature it is *eo ipso* "natural." "There is nothing that is supernatural but God alone; everything besides Him is from and subject to the state of nature. . . . There is nothing supernatural in [Redemption] or belonging to it but that supernatural love and wisdom which brought it forth, presides over it and will direct it till Christ as a second Adam has removed and extinguished all that evil which the first Adam brought into human nature" (p. 444).

Law perceived that to reduce righteousness to an imputed quality prepared the ground for setting up a *natural* religion next to one so tenuously linked to nature. Christianity itself is the true and only religion of nature. "For a religion is the one, true religion of nature when it has everything in it that our natural state stands in need of" (p. 453). I have referred to Law because he saw the problems created by a forensic theory of redemption, after they had had occasion to develop and contribute to the religious crisis of the eighteenth century. In teaching against that theory he returned to the fundamental purpose of the Reformation, namely, to restore the unity of nature and grace lost by the distinction between the orders of nature and the supernatural.

The early humanists' attempt to recapture the lost unity of nature and grace seldom receives the attention it deserves. Past interpretations have tended to dismiss the entire movement as a return to classical paganism, modified by some half-hearted compromises between an undogmatic Christianity and an adjusted Neoplatonism. The efforts of at least some of its religious writers to forge a tighter link between revelation and what experience or philosophy teaches us about human nature deserve to be taken more seriously. Some of the early humanists considered the pre-Christian religious aspira-

---

6. William Law, *The Spirit of Love,* Dialogue III, in *The Classics of Western Spirituality* (New York: Paulist Press, 1980), p. 439.

tions of the classical writers fully continuous with their Christian fulfillment.

Marsilio Ficino's *Theologia platonica* interprets Plato's *eros* as prefiguring the harmony of grace and nature to which the Christian aspires. His rethinking of Christian love situates the Florentine humanist closer to the Greek Fathers than to Plato or Plotinus.[7] Pico della Mirandola likewise asserts the priority of love: "As long as we dwell in this world, imprisoned in the life of the senses, it is through love more than through reason that we are able to grasp God."[8]

Rather than using the classical philosophers for spare parts in constructing an exclusively Christian theology, as Scholastics tended to do, Pico and Ficino placed Plato and Plotinus on an equal footing with the prophets. They assumed the existence of an uninterrupted continuity between creation and redemption, and hence also between the noble philosophy of the pre-Christian classics and revealed faith. If Christian revelation is true, it must be fully compatible with the great teachings of Antiquity. The Platonic theory of forms provided religious artists of the Renaissance with a justification for fully displaying the natural world in such a way that, in an upward movement, it surpassed its own finitude. In the visible the artist seeks the invisible. No one pursued this religious naturalism more consistently than Michelangelo, who, though coming at the end of the Renaissance, perhaps most perfectly realized its early religious ideal.[9]

---

7. In distinguishing love from *libido*, Ficino places himself in the medieval tradition of courtly love in Italy represented by Brunetto Latini, Guido Cavalcanti, and Dante. Festugière suggests a direct acquaintance with the theoretical *Flos Amoris* which circulated under Boccaccio's name.

8. Pico della Mirandola, *Opera* (Basel, 1576), p. 250.

9. Having often been admitted in his adolescence to the Medici Academy, where Pico and Ficino exposed their theories, Michelangelo had over the years deepened a Neoplatonic aesthetics of form into a religious vision. In the light of this vision the artist had become dissatisfied with the self-contained finite form and had increasingly attempted to convey a transcendent openness to his sculpture and painting.

Still, Christian humanism failed in fully integrating the disparate elements from which it built its synthesis. Pre-Christian antiquity and Christian revelation intrinsically differed from each other. Their accommodation had to be constantly reexamined. As neither Renaissance artists nor later humanists did so, it developed into a nonreligious naturalism.

Jansenism and the Baroque

A third attempt to restore the lost unity of grace and nature resulted in one of the most complex theological systems Western thought has ever devised. It was also one of the most elusive. Though attacked, criticized, and repeatedly condemned, it was never definitively refuted. It started from the nominalist concept of God's *potentia absoluta*. This included the *possibility* of a *pure nature,* that is, a human nature without "supernatural" gifts, grace, or participation in divine life. Until the sixteenth century this fiction had remained a mere working hypothesis for developing theories of grace. In the sixteenth century some theologians began to assume it to be a reality in its own right.

Two Flemish theologians, Baius and Jansenius, perceived how much the new theology of nature and grace had deviated from a tradition established since Augustine. Baius attempted to restore that tradition, but ended up with a peculiar mixture of a most untraditional "naturalism" and an equally new supernaturalism. On the basis of a well-known passage in Augustine, Baius denied that human nature had been fully formed until it received the *forma filiorum Dei*— the original state of justice—which later Scholasticism, in order to stress its gratuitousness, had come to call "supernatural." For Baius, then, grace is a *demand* of nature and God's image in grace is the natural image of the soul. Adam by his "natural" powers not only desired but also claimed a divine destination. Thus Baius with one bold stroke united what for centuries had been sundered. But the problems return with his description of the fall. Once deprived of its original justice, human nature itself breaks down to a truncated reality. Since grace formed an *essential* part of nature, the loss of original justice rendered nature intrinsically incapable of natural goodness. Even a habit of accomplishing one's duty becomes vitiated by a general orientation toward concupiscence rather than toward charity. The virtues of this fallen nature, then, are nothing but what Augustine called *splendida vitia*.

Jansenius, his admiring student and successor at the Louvain faculty, elaborated these insights into a more comprehensive system that he presented as Augustine's theology of grace. He gave a pessimistic twist as well as a greater consistency to his mentor's theses. At the same time he avoided the "Pelagian" features of Baius's theology, which Rome had condemned. He repeated that God *morally owed* it to an intellectual creature to call it to the highest form of spiritual life. In his original state Adam needed no "grace." His very nature was grace. But by the fall nature had been permanently crippled, and grace had disappeared altogether. If grace was to be restored, it would not so much assist nature as become a substitute for it. Once humanity had turned away from God (in the original sin) it could be transformed only by ceasing to function naturally.

Henceforth God's decree alone could save the elect by steering them "almost irresistibly" toward salvation. Jansenism remains hard to refute on its own terms, even though there was no lack of trying by the Roman Curia, which condemned it five times over. It owed its power of resistance to the fact that, more than any other theological system, it consistently drew the conclusions from the modern premises: the separation of grace from nature and of nature from grace. I have discussed the details of this protracted battle in *Passage to Modernity* (1993).

All attempts to regain the unity lost at the dawn of the modern age failed. As the idea of nature grew more and more "secular," Christian faith became increasingly remote from ordinary life. Before concluding this chapter, however, I must at least mention the short-lived but truly remarkable reintegration of religion and culture achieved during the Baroque period in some parts of Europe. The Baroque was far more than an artistic style. It consisted in a new way of thinking and feeling, of artistic expression and social structure, which, while rarely innovative in theology, reunited nature and grace in the practical order. The human person remained at the center of the world stage, which he had come to occupy at the beginning of the modern age. He viewed himself as the main actor. Yet at the same time he recognized that his power depended on a transcendent source. He lived in a spiritual universe that had two centers: one human and one transcendent. Sacred art expressed this awareness of a dual center in the oval shape of the Baroque vault, which pulled the closed Renaissance circle apart; in the convoluted columns that seemed to ascend beyond the finitude of the straight classical ones; and in the diagonal line that dynamically drove the lower parts of a canvas or sculptured surface beyond the confines of the represented space. The abundance of saints and angels rising in ascending circles along the cupolas of Baroque churches fulfilled the function of mediating the terrestrial with the celestial realm.

Nor did the mediated vision return the Baroque to a medieval cosmology, in which the earth stood at the physical center of the universe. Copernicus, Pope Paul III, and Galileo, as well as the Jesuits of the Roman College, understood what Pico della Mirandola had written, namely, that the person occupies not the physical but the spiritual center of the universe. Indeed, to the Baroque mind the physical world seemed infinitely expandable. Epics glorified the discovery of new worlds, while elaborate liturgies, majestic architecture, and ambitious theater productions celebrated the splendor of a resacralized universe.

This magnificent synthesis was to break apart after a relatively short time, under the weight of the very tensions to which it owed its uniquely dynamic quality. It fractured all the more quickly since the Baroque had neglected to integrate the most significant achievement of modern culture—the scientific revolution. It did not obstruct it, as Catholic thought tended to do in the nineteenth century. But neither did the Catholic Church incorporate it in its evangelization. Apprehensive after the continuing loss of so many members in northern and central Europe, she increasingly adopted a policy of caution rather than of theoretical adjustment to the intellectual demands of the new age. Even today she still has not achieved an intellectual synthesis of faith with modern thought, as the constant tensions between theology and modern science indicate. The short period of the Baroque was the last time the two were united.

chapter T H R E E

The Crisis of the Enlightenment

Having sketched a general picture of modern culture as distinct from that of the preceding era and more specifically of the transformation of the religious consciousness at the beginning of the modern epoch, I now turn to that second wave of modernity, which occurred during the period between the end of the Thirty Years' War (1648) and the French Revolution (1789).

The Second Stage of Modern Culture

The three stages of modern culture—humanism and the Renaissance, the Enlightenment, and the period following the French Revolution—shared some basic principles. Yet their relation was never one in which the earlier stage "caused" the later one. Each presented a creative event in its own right, even though the later could not have emerged without the earlier. Nor can the periods be reduced to a common denominator. Each expressed a different innovative impulse, yet together they constituted a single cultural epoch.

Descartes introduced a new method for establishing epistemic certainty by making the object of knowledge conform to the mind's own laws. He thereby attempted to overcome the skepticism that was partly a result of the nominalist thought of the preceding two centuries. British thinkers reacted differently. With the nominalists they excluded an a priori approach to truth and turned to methodically conducted observation. Together, the two approaches—the mathematical and the empirical—prepared the way for the scientific revolution and determined the intellectual course of the Enlightenment.

I realize that it is hazardous to speak of "the" Enlightenment, when the movement differed so much from one area to another. Is a general discussion even justified? Despite the diversity, we are justified in treating the Enlightenment as one movement because of the interaction of the various manifestations of what appear to have been common causes. At least they resulted in building a cultural complex with some features that distinguish it from the preceding as well as from the following periods. France and England, the two countries of origin, produced almost simultaneously men of exceptional genius who could not fail to exchange ideas with one another. Later, during the second half of the eighteenth century, German thinkers of considerable originality, such as Lessing, Kant, and Herder, developed ideas in dialectical opposition to the prevailing ones which in turn fertilized the French and the English. Thus, through continuous influences, various intellectual strands gradually coalesced into what at least in retrospect may be considered a single, complex culture.

The Enlightenment enjoys no high reputation in our age. We consider its thinking one-sided, its feeling inauthentic. All too often it sacrificed content to form, concreteness to abstraction, individuality to universality. Its claim that the new era, concluding centuries of obscurantism and superstition, introduced at last a millennium of freedom and progress sounds preposterous to us. Despite the presence of some great painters, such as Watteau, Chardin, and La Tour in France and Gainesborough and Reynolds in England, the Enlightenment produced no artists comparable to the giants of the sixteenth and seventeenth centuries.

Only music enjoyed a glorious season. Yet, as have I tried to show in *The Enlightenment and the Intellectual Foundations of Modern Culture,*

Handel, Bach, and Haydn continued to draw their inspiration from the culture of the Baroque. Mozart, despite an occasional bow to Freemasonry, paid little attention to the new ideas. All of this induced Baron Grimm to write in his influential bulletin about cultural life in Paris: "To me, it seems that the eighteenth century has surpassed all others in the praise it has bestowed upon itself. But I am far from imagining that we have reached an age of reason."

But the Enlightenment accomplished pioneering work in science, in history, and especially in philosophy. Gibbon, Montesquieu, Voltaire, and Herder initiated modern history writing. Spinoza, Leibniz, Locke, Berkeley, and Hume, the great philosophers of the Enlightenment, tower high above the thinkers of the preceding century, with the sole exception of Descartes, who influenced all of them. Kant still continues to determine the philosophical reflection of our time. In this contrast between a remarkable upsurge of science and philosophy and a relative decrease of artistic creativity, the Enlightenment reveals itself to be in the first place a critical culture.

In this respect it was extremely consistent—indeed, so much so that it prepared the ground for its own critique. When we today attack the Enlightenment for its one-sidedness, we do so by principles formulated and justified by Enlightenment thought. That thought still defines much of contemporary culture, both in projecting its enormous possibilities and in forecasting its unprecedented problems. For that reason the Enlightenment continues to present a challenge to contemporary thinking. In the present chapter I shall merely outline some of the conditions that made the Enlightenment possible and that defined its general direction. In the next chapter I shall address more specifically its impact on religion.

The Enlightenment

Each culture adheres to a number of mostly implicit ideas that determine its entire course. They are usually conceived at the time of its early maturity or at the occasion of significant changes in its development. I suggested in the first chapter that the oldest permanent idea in Western culture may well have been that of form. We find it expressed in Greek poetry, art, and philosophy. For the Greeks of the classical age, the true reality of things consisted in their form. Whatever cannot be clearly circumscribed must be relegated to the not-fully-real realm of the indefinite. It was on the idea of form that the Greek primacy of reason rested.

That idea assumed a fundamentally different meaning in early modern thought. While originally *form* had been inherent in a *given* nature, it later became an ideal to be pursued by human endeavor. Enlightenment theory radicalized those changes. This appears most evident in the theory of art. Critics continued to repeat the ancient rule that art must imitate nature. But the modern came to understand "imitation" in a manner that had little to do with representing nature *as it in fact appears*. The model to be followed was *la belle nature,* not nature as given, but nature as embellished by the artist until it corresponded to his or her own ideal. The change gradually led art to be conceived in terms of *self-expression*. Enlightenment aesthetics thereby differs substantially from ancient and even early modern aesthetics. While for the latter the aesthetic focus was outside the mind, Enlightenment aesthetics located it *within* the mind. Anthony Ashley Cooper, third Earl of Shaftesbury, wrote at the beginning of the eighteenth century: "Nothing affects the heart like that which is purely from itself, and of its own nature; such as the beauty of sentiments, the grace of actions, the turn of characters, and the proportions and features of the human mind."[1] The artist is a second creator, a "Prometheus under Zeus," who expresses his inner life more than he imitates nature. Since nature itself is creative, the artist remains most faithful to her example when releasing the creative powers within his own nature. Aesthetic form consists in *form-giving,* in "the beautifying, not the beautified."[2] The aesthetic ideal does not reside in a sphere beyond ordinary reality (as it did for Plato); it originates in *the*

---

1. Anthony Cooper, Lord Shaftesbury, "Advice to an Author," in *Characteristics of Men, Manners, Opinions, Times,* ed. John M. Robertson (Gloucester, Mass.: Peter Smith, 1963), vol. 1, Part I, Section 3, p. 136.

2. "The Moralists," in *Characteristics,* vol. 2, Part III, Section 2, p. 131.

mind's reflection on the physical world. The artist's intuition recreates the physical form into one expressive of the mind's own nature.

In ethics a similar displacement occurred. Most moralists agreed that human nature constitutes the ground of morality. They also admitted that this nature forms part of an all-comprehensive order. But the concept of natural law, through which that order had formerly been thought to rule morality, received a different meaning. What previously had been considered to be grounded in a divinely established order now came to depend exclusively on human reason. Kant eliminated the last remnants of any pre-given element in the moral law when he claimed that good and evil do not exist *before* the law of reason—they are constituted *in* and *through* that law. Nor can we ever appeal to any higher authority than that law of reason.

In England a different reinterpretation of morality led to equally significant results. For Shaftesbury, "moral sense" consisted in a direct intuition of the *good,* related to the aesthetic intuition of the beautiful. Moral feelings require no additional justification: they are self-sufficient. The center of the moral consciousness consists in a feeling of sympathy for others. Later, the feeling of self-love was added to it. The two were assumed to remain harmoniously united.

Out of the morality of feelings arose the idea of "the beautiful soul." Rousseau in his *Julie, ou la nouvelle Héloise* (1761) described it as a moral attitude that, beyond conventions and obligations, allows itself to be directed solely by "the law of the heart." At the end Julie, the heroine of the novel, marries the elderly man her father had chosen for her, but allows her lover to live with them in a chaste relationship. By thus following the law of the heart, they hope to return morality to its original purity and to avoid the hypocritical conventions of society.

Schiller in his essay *On Grace and Dignity* (*Über Anmut und Würde*) (1793) endowed this ideal of the beautiful soul with the qualities of grace and dignity. Inspired by the ancient Greek notion of *kalokagathon,* he argued that true moral goodness cannot but be gracious. He thus combined the stern principle of Kant's categorical imperative in *The Metaphysics of Morals* with the aesthetic ideal of his *Critique of Judgment.* Only a person who knows how to translate an inner moral attitude into gracious conduct can be called fully moral. In such a one the moral disposition has become so natural that moral acts effortlessly flow forth from it. "We call a soul beautiful when the moral feeling of all experiences of the person attain such a degree, that she may leave the direction of will to her natural inclinations without running the risk of colliding with her consciousness. Hence with a beautiful soul not the singular acts are moral, but the entire character is."[3]

Goethe also, in the "Confessions of a Beautiful Soul" (*Bekenntnisse einer schönen Seele*), the sixth book of *Wilhelm Meister's Apprentice Years* (*Wilhelm Meisters Lehrjahre*) (1795), expresses respect for the nobility of the beautiful soul. At the same time, one senses a certain irony in his description of a life that often avoids confronting the harsh reality of everyday existence. The story concludes with the heroine's ambiguous confession: "Nothing appears to me in the form of a law; an impulse leads me and directs me ever on the right way. I freely follow my inclinations and know neither restrictions nor regrets."

Eventually the ethics of altruistic feelings hardened into a calculating utilitarianism. Good then becomes whatever one estimates will benefit the greatest number of people. The morality of acts thereby depends not on the nature of the acts but upon their consequences. Obviously this position, even more than that of moral feelings, stands at the opposite side of Kant's ethical imperative. Nonetheless, both agree with Kant's ideal of moral autonomy. Moral law as well as moral feelings spring from the same source: the human mind, ordering through reason or manifest in feelings. Even Kant's followers allowed moral sense a guiding role in human conduct. To one who has long obeyed the rule of law, the gentle voice of moral sense might suffice for doing his duty.

The changes in aesthetic theories and moral attitudes went hand in hand with religious transformations. The church historian Ernst Troeltsch states that in the eighteenth century European culture

---

3. *Über Anmut und Würde,* in *Schillers Werke* (Weimar: Nationalausgabe, 1962), vol. 20, p. 287.

ceased to be Christian. To be sure, the great majority of Europeans remained faithful to their religious beliefs and practices. Even radical thinkers continued to profess some loyalty to traditional beliefs. But the very nature of religion had changed. The *philosophes* considered God the necessary cause of motion in the mechanistic world system. They also were convinced that moral rules needed a reliable source of reward and punishment to be effective. Some even felt that a general providence directed the course of history. In the next chapter, we shall see how these positions came to be undermined by the science and the ethical theories of the eighteenth century. In the present one, we merely focus on the cultural conditions that made the more radical religious changes possible.

One that played a crucial role consisted in the application of the methods of historical criticism to Scripture. Early humanists, beginning with Lorenzo Valla and Erasmus, had spent considerable efforts in retrieving the original text of the New Testament, which had been buried under the layers of questionable traditions and poorly copied manuscripts. But rarely had they or later philologists questioned the meaning of the text they so laboriously restored. Catholics as well as Protestants assumed that a literal reading was imperative for preserving the truth of the New Testament. With respect to the Old Testament, questions about Moses' authorship of the Pentateuch and about the religious significance of some of the later writings had been raised for some time. No one knew what to do with some of the historical narratives of the Old Testament.

Before Spinoza, few had ever undertaken an interpretation of the text that went beyond a literal, historical reading. In his *Tractatus Theologico-Politicus,* the Dutch philosopher drove a wedge between the meaning of the sacred text and its historical accuracy. The meaning depended not on the veracity of the reporting, he claimed, but on the writer's intention. That intention, according to Spinoza, consisted entirely in an exhortation to obedience, which was to prepare the Hebrews for attaining their historical destiny. As for the historical reliability, that was entirely dependent on the author's intention.

A succession of increasingly radical reinterpretations followed Spinoza's work. In his posthumous papers the German Orientalist Hermann Samuel Reimarus extended the critique of the Bible to the

New Testament. Gotthold Ephraim Lessing published fragments of these papers for the purpose of raising even more fundamental questions. In light of the distinction between necessary truths of reason and contingent truths of facts, he critically reexamined the conclusions derived from the historical reports of the Gospel. "What does it mean to accept an historical proposition as true? To believe an historical truth? Does it mean anything other than this: to accept this proposition, this truth as valid? To jump with that historical truth [of Christ's resurrection] to a quite different class of truths, and to demand of me that I should form all my metaphysical and moral ideals accordingly; to alter all my fundamental ideas of the nature of the Godhead because I cannot set any credible testimony against the resurrection of Christ: if that is not a *metabasis eis allo genos,* I do not know what Aristotle meant by this phrase."[4]

Hume in his *Natural History of Religion* approached the question from a different angle. On the basis of a presumed acquaintance with the religious feelings of premodern peoples, he concluded that all could be reduced to an emotion of fear. Humans possess no innate awareness of or respect for a transcendent power. Nor does the acceptance of such powers heighten the moral sense, an idea that for the *philosophes* had been the principal, if not the only justification of religious faith. Quite the opposite occurs: ritualism appears to dispense people from their moral obligations.

From all sides faith was under siege. Its predicament was, together with the drastic changes in moral theory, responsible for what has been called "the crisis of modern consciousness."[5] In the next chapter we shall discuss the actual changes in religion. Before doing so, however, let us briefly consider whether the fundamental trans-

---

4. Gotthold Ephraim Lessing, "On the Proof of the Spirit and Power," in *Lessing's Theological Writings,* trans. Henry Chadwick (Stanford, Calif.: Stanford University Press, 1957), p. 54.

5. This is the title of Paul Hazard's well-known study, *La crise de la conscience européenne* (1935). In English, *The European Mind, 1680–1715,* trans. J. Lewis May (London: Hollis and Carter, 1953).

formations that occurred in the eighteenth century justify referring to them as a cultural crisis.

The Enlightenment as a Cultural Crisis

When a society no longer recognizes itself in the ideals that have traditionally directed it, and yet its members continue to feel beholden to them, a crisis originates. Hegel called this state of cultural ambivalence *alienation* (*Entfremdung*), a term that was to feature prominently in the revolutionary jargon of his unorthodox followers, Feuerbach and Marx. In the *Phenomenology of Spirit,* he presented the entire Enlightenment as a state of profound social alienation. *Insight* and *faith,* Greek rationality and Christian faith, the two principles that had been fundamental in shaping Western culture, became engaged in a life-and-death struggle. Rationality hardened into rationalism; faith weakened into a belief incapable of justification.

Since Hegel's assessment we have had occasion to reflect more deeply on the Enlightenment's theoretical and practical principles in the retrospective light of our later experience. In his *Philosophical Discourse of Modernity* the German philosopher Jürgen Habermas has attempted to revalidate the original project of the Enlightenment, which, in his opinion, had been deflected from its course by the development of post-Kantian thought. In the theory of the Absolute Spirit, he claims, Hegel erected a pseudo-religion, which obscured and retarded the original program of human emancipation. Habermas's interpretation of the *Aufklärung* reduces an extraordinarily complex phenomenon to a project of political emancipation, while overlooking the ethical and aesthetic factors that played a determining role in the movement. To resume the description of the Enlightenment as a struggle between insight and faith, one might say that he has eliminated faith altogether, as all Marxists have done.

Habermas is undoubtedly right that the Enlightenment continues to challenge us today. We have not yet succeeded in grasping its full implications. It may also be true that the Enlightenment project was prematurely abandoned. But contrary to his claim, I believe that it was not so much the execution as the conception of the project that had remained incomplete. The concept of social emancipation alone, without any definition of its goals and restrictions, rests on an abstract, somewhat utopian idea of rationality. In my view, a broader idea of reason is needed, one in which rationality is conceived as being in accordance with the order inherent in the nature of things.

In conceiving of rationality exclusively as an attribute of the human mind, independent of any ulterior norm, the Enlightenment unduly narrowed the ideal of emancipation. Rationalism radicalized what for Descartes had been an intellectual experiment, which he himself qualified by his theory of truth as being conditioned by divine illumination. (I do not consider that theory to provide an adequate interpretation of knowledge, but at least it shows Descartes' concern for widening the notion of truth beyond the limits of the human mind.) The Enlightenment transformed that experiment into a comprehensive emancipation program.

The danger in restricting reason to the human mind is that it reduces reason to an instrument in the hands of human subjects. *Theoria* then comes to stand in the service of an all too easily self-directed *praxis*. The goals set by a program of rationalist universality seldom reflect the concrete order of reality, but rather reflect those set by *particular* interests. We tend to think of rationalism and utilitarianism as opposites: they are, in fact, twins born of the same parent, namely, a reduced concept of reason. Not fortuitously does Hegel, in his famous description of the Enlightenment as the age of abstract reason, view utilitarianism as its primary effect. The reduction of rationality to the abstract universal of logic explains how ideals of rationality could be very unfairly imposed as allegedly universal systems of well-being, all in the name of reason. Examples abound: universal human rights combined with slavery, a universal ideal of democracy inflicted upon societies governed by different political principles, an abstract theory of social equality exported to all parts of the world, and so on.

One might object that the empiricism which dominated British philosophy during the period of the Enlightenment does not labor under the problems of rationalist universalism. Here the content of knowledge derived entirely from sensations and reflections. Yet on the basic issue, that the norms of reason come exclusively from the mind, the two systems remain in full accord. The root of the rationalist problem consists not in the creation of a false universalism, nor in the exclusive reliance on a priori methods of reasoning, but in the attribution of the sources of reason exclusively to the human mind. Nor was the empiricist school less pragmatic than the rationalist one. Quite the contrary! John Mill and Jeremy Bentham, illustrious members of that school, were the ones who provided the philosophical justification of utilitarianism. Histories of modern thought justifiably classify both schools under the heading *Rationalism,* because they stem from a common subjective source.

The consequences of this rationalism cannot be overestimated. Reacting against the French universalism, which the revolutionary armies had exported all over Europe, the formerly conquered nations strongly reasserted their sovereignty and acrimoniously defended their political independence. An aggressive nationalism developed and continued to grow throughout the nineteenth century. It exploded in the First World War. In the wake of this disaster, the universalist movement of Russian communism became a threatening power, while the violent nationalism in a defeated Germany led to the Second World War.

Leninism, the youngest and most radical child of the Enlightenment, intended to replace historical traditions by a homogenizing project of human engineering. Over against it, a racist nationalism recognized only the nation's own right. We tend to see them as irreconcilable opposites, yet both Soviet Communism and National Socialism derive from a common philosophical ancestor, a subjectivist concept of reason. Nor should we hold the traditional principle of rationality responsible for the politics of raw power, unrestricted social libertarianism, and ecologically destructive economies, as some postmodern writers tend to do. All such modes of conduct conflict with reason and are due to the distorted, anthropocentric, pragmatic and utilitarian readings of the principle of reason.

Despite these problems, the Enlightenment's attempt to establish the priority of reason (albeit in an adulterated form) has left a number of permanent benefits. Among them are strong support for freedom and democracy, an expressive conception of art, and non-authoritarian theories of morality. Today we particularly honor its declaration of human rights. However shaky the juridical ground on which that declaration rests, reason does indeed entitle each person to certain basic human rights. Similarly, the notion of a social contract, despite attacks on its "fictional foundation" by Hume, Burke, and others, rightly replaces the self-justifying authoritarian structures of political institutions by an obligation to respond to the reasonable needs and expectations of the concrete community. Time and again, we find the humanitarian concerns of the Enlightenment surpassing the dubious arguments that had been used to justify them.

Even the Enlightenment's justly criticized position on religion has left a valuable legacy. Religious tolerance and, indispensable to it, separation between church and state, respect for the individual conscience, and rejection of political coercion, social pressure, and cultural prejudice—these have become nonnegotiable items of Western belief. The historical critique of biblical texts at last forced the Church to qualify its unconditional literalism. Hume's attack on the traditional arguments of the existence of God and Lessing's exposure of the weakness of the historical ones for the truth of the Christian faith proved the inadequacy of a rationalist approach in discussing transcendent principles. The critique proved painful, particularly in the sarcastic form in which it was often administered. Yet it drove religion back to its spiritual home and prepared it for the even more severe attacks of the nineteenth-century scientists. We fully acknowledge the benefits the primacy of the principles of rationality and freedom have brought us. The Enlightenment has made us what we are today. How can we profit from its lessons while avoiding its excesses?

chapter F O U R

On the Intellectual Sources of Modern Atheism

Atheism and Deism

The term atheism is not new. Those who attempted to re-think the nature of transcendence have always been called atheists. Socrates was branded with the invective term for undermining the polytheist religion of his time and so, in a different way, was Epicurus. Yet both believed in God or the gods. Closer to our own time the pious Spinoza was charged with atheism for having articulated the relation between transcendence and immanence in concepts that varied from the traditional ones. The stigma adhered to his name throughout the eighteenth century. Lessing's reputation as a religious deist changed overnight when Jacobi revealed his Spinozistic leanings. The controversy about Spinoza ended in the *Atheismusstreit* in which Fichte lost his chair at the University of Jena.

The "atheism" dealt with in this chapter was both more radical and more comprehensive. It consisted not in a *shift* of the relation between immanence and transcendence, but in a gradual evanescence of the very idea of transcendence. Unlike earlier "atheism," it failed to replace what it abolished. It was in fact the outcome of an intellectual movement derived from Christian theological assumptions. By one-sidedly emphasizing the idea of God's omnipotence, the nominalist theology in the late Middle Ages had ruptured the intimate bond that had linked Creator and creation. In disturbing the harmonious relation between reason and revelation it caused endless polemics, which eventually broke up the unity of Christendom altogether. When the protracted religious wars of the sixteenth century finally forced Europeans to search for a new spiritual unity, the compromise that emerged bore the marks of the theological controversies of the previous century. The original attempts to restore religious peace preserved the theological categories of nature and grace, of reason and revelation. But reason provided the basis for all further discussion. This first led to the birth of a new kind of deism.

Deism had existed for a long time, longer in Islam than in Christianity. The ninth-century Baghdad theologian al-Kindi had argued the rational and hence universal nature of the prophetic revelation. Al-Farabi (d. 950) and Ibn Sina (Avicenna) (d. 1037) had professed similar beliefs. The idea that the existence of God could be reached by human reason had been implicit in Thomas Aquinas. A number of early Renaissance thinkers, such as Nicholas of Cusa, Marsilio Ficino, Pico della Mirandola, and Jean Bodin, had explicitly accepted it. They all asserted that the human mind *naturally* longs for God and that this desire must come from a divine source. Far from excluding revelation, many attributed this natural religion to an aboriginal revelation made at the beginning of the human race. This allegedly primeval revelation was thought to have left some inner awareness of God. Some claimed to have detected vestiges of an aboriginal monotheism in Egyptian, Greek, and Roman polytheism. As late as the eighteenth century, the Cambridge Platonists still regarded it as the foundation of an innate religious disposition.

The deists of the eighteenth century promoted a different kind of deism. According to them, reason alone, independently of *any* revelation, establishes the necessary and sufficient principle of transcendence needed for the support of morality and the foundation of cosmology. They bolstered their argument by Roman writers, such as Varro and Cicero, in whose works Christians, ever since Augustine, had found an arsenal of weapons against polytheism and atheism. But they did so for the purpose of establishing a natural theology that could dispense with revelation altogether. The new deism became a rival religion. Its principles included the existence of a Creator, source of cosmic motion, who rewards good and punishes evil, and whose providence guides history toward a progress of morality and culture.

Although it claimed to be a product of reason alone, this deism was in fact the result of a filtering process that had strained off all historical and dogmatic data from Christian theology and retained only that minimum which, by eighteenth-century standards, reason demands. It appeared to be more an attenuated version of Christianity than a religion of pure reason. Its idea of God contained enough remnants of its origin to be recognizable as the ghost of the Christian God. It was a rationalist abstraction of an unacknowledged Christian idea. "I know of no greater tribute ever paid to the God of Christianity," Etienne Gilson quipped, "than His survival in this idea, maintained against Christianity itself and on the strength of pure natural reason."[1]

The earliest protagonists of this rationalist deism continued to admit revelation as possible and as even practically necessary because of the weakness of human reason. Fausto Sozzini, to whom friends as well as enemies traced the deist lineage, and Matthew Tindal, author of *Christianity as Old as Creation* (1730), the "Bible of the deists," accepted a primeval revelation, the core of which Christianity shared with reason and with all other religions. But the text most responsible for the spread of rationalist deism in Britain and France, Locke's *On the Reasonableness of Christianity* (1695), was in fact a work of Christian piety, written by a believing Christian. What earned it a place in deist literature—a place Locke himself firmly refused—was the thesis that the content of revealed religion is com-

---

1. Etienne Gilson, *God and Philosophy* (New Haven: Yale University Press, 1941), p. 106.

patible with reason and that the credibility of its revealed authority can be rationally justified. The deist appropriation, then, seems unjustified.

Still, Locke's interpreters were not entirely wrong in finding an essential principle of the deist position hidden in his work, namely, that reason must be the final judge of the Gospel's truth. This thesis reversed the traditional priority of divine revelation with respect to human reason. Reason now must provide the sole foundation of religious beliefs, including that of any possible revelation. As a result, the "arguments" for the existence of God assumed an unprecedented importance, both among believers and among deists. While earlier philosophical theology had merely "justified" revelation in the light of reason, deism required that reason first establish the *foundation* of faith.

The deist inversion appeared nowhere more clearly than in the reduction of religion to the domain of morals. With characteristic assurance Voltaire defined natural religion as "the principles of morals common to the human race."[2] In ethics, the person takes the initiative; in religion as traditionally understood, the initiative comes from God. "A religious *ethos* superseded the religious *pathos* which had motivated the preceding centuries of religious controversy."[3] Religion had scarcely any function left but that of sanctioning morality. D'Alembert declared in the *Discours préliminaire de l'Encyclopédie*: "One would do a great service to mankind if one could make men forget the dogmas; if one would simply preach them a God who rewards and punishes and who frowns on superstition, who detests intolerance and expects no other cult of man than mutual love and support."[4] Voltaire measured the virtue of religion by its use to society.[5]

---

2. Voltaire, *Eléments de philosophie de Newton* (1738), in *Oeuvres* (Paris, 1785), vol. 63, Part I, ch. 6.

3. Ernst Cassirer, *The Philosophy of the Enlightenment,* trans. Fritz C. A. Koeln and James P. Pettegrove (Princeton: Princeton University Press, 1951), p. 164.

4. Jean le Rond d'Alembert, "Discours préliminaire," *Encyclopédie* (ed. Picaret), p. xv.

5. Voltaire, *Eléments de philosophie de Newton.*

For deists, religion was the conclusion of an argument, rather than a revealed *given,* which reason may subsequently attempt to justify. They overlooked the fact that philosophy *encounters* the idea of God; it does not invent or deduce it.[6] In Thomas Aquinas's view, God had not even been an object of metaphysics. He admitted, to be sure, that philosophy necessitates the acceptance of a transcendent principle. But only revelation identifies this principle with the Christian God. Each of Thomas's five *ways,* by modern readers incorrectly interpreted as "arguments," concludes with the words: *Et hoc est quod omnes vocant Deum,* long before all the necessary elements of a formal argument are in place. The *Summa Theologiae,* like many other Scholastic works, is a theological text composed with the assistance of philosophical concepts. Deists, however, claimed to deduce God's existence as well as God's attributes from religiously neutral premises. Their natural religion, though it owed its origin to the Christian idea of God, pretended to rest on reason alone.

Creation and Causality

Eighteenth-century deists derived the idea of God so exhaustively from reason that the distinction between immanence and transcendence lost much of its meaning. Thus they paved the way to atheism. Still, their strong insistence on distinguishing themselves from atheism raises the question: What, then, was the factor in modern thought that immediately led to atheism? I have no doubt that it was the identification of God's creative act with one of efficient causality.

The modern notion of causality substantially differed from the ancient and medieval one. Early Christian theologians were wont to contrast God's creative act to that of the Demiurge in Plato's *Timaeus.* God had made the world out of nothing (*de nihilo*), while the Demiurge had used preexisting matter (*chora*). But Plato's *Timaeus* is not

---

6. Henry Duméry, *Le problème de Dieu* (Paris: Desclée De Brouwer, 1975), p. 15.

about creation but about the metaphysical principles of *Being*. The Demiurge is not a Creator but a mythical figure that illustrates the active combination of those metaphysical principles. Most importantly, for Plato, Aristotle, and Plotinus, efficient causality is by no means the only or even the primary form of causality. Causality for them could also be formal or final. What modern philosophy attributed to efficient causality appeared in Plato in the form of participation, a mode of formal causality.

There appears to be little doubt, then, that the early Christian Fathers, in their polemics with ancient philosophy, misinterpreted Plato's thought when they opposed a creation *from nothing* to one *from primary matter*. Later theology corrected this narrowly one-sided interpretation. Christians had always considered the bond between God and creation as more intimate than one of efficient causality. After Neoplatonic philosophy began to influence first the Eastern and, since Victorinus and Augustine, also the Western Fathers, they increasingly turned to the Platonic doctrine of participation for interpreting the relation between God and created beings.

The rediscovery of Aristotle's *Physics* and *Metaphysics,* which presented the Prime Mover as cause of all power, restored the theory of efficient causality to a dominant position in the theology of creation. Without going into the various factors that played a role in this process (I have discussed some in *Passage to Modernity*), I shall mention only the following. St. Thomas continues to hesitate between Plato's participation and Aristotle's notion of efficient causality for describing the relation between God and the creature.[7]

The following passage of the *Summa Theologiae* (I, q.8, a.1) appears to emphasize the intimate presence of the Creator in the creature: "Being is innermost in each thing and most fundamentally present within all things, since it is formal in respect of everything found in a thing. . . . Hence it must be that God is in all things, and

---

7. Cf. Cornelio Fabro, *La nozione metafisica di participazione secondo S. Tomasso d'Aquino* (Brescia, 1939), and L. B. Geiger, *La participation dans la philosophie de St. Thomas* (Paris, 1942).

innermostly." Nonetheless, in defining the nature of this divine immanence, Thomas claims that it must consist in a relation of causal dependence. This causal dependence seems further defined in terms of efficient causality, for in the same article he explains: "An agent must be joined to that wherein it acts immediately, and touch it by its power; hence it is proved in the *Physics* (VII, 2) that the thing moved and the mover must be together. Now since God is Being itself by his own essence, created being must be his proper effect; just as to ignite is the proper effect of fire." Thomas thereby appears to give less than what the words "innermost presence" promised.

After I had written my interpretation of this text, an auditor at the Erasmus lectures, Harold Ernst, brought another passage from the *Summa* to my attention, which attributes the causality of fire in the sense of participation (I, q.3, a.4, ad 3). "Just as that which has fire but is not itself fire is on fire by participation, so that which has being but is not being, is a being by participation." This clear statement makes a reading of the idea of creation in the *Summa Theologiae* exclusively in terms of efficient causality at least doubtful. In the earlier text, however, Thomas refers to Aristotle's *Physics,* which definitely deals with efficient causality. To me, the difference between the two passages appearing at close proximity to one another seems to indicate Thomas's uncertainty on the matter in this later work. Still, we ought to keep in mind that Aristotle's efficient causality essentially differs, precisely on the immanence of the cause in the effect, from the later mechanistic conception.

In late medieval thought, divine causality became increasingly conceived as an external source. The process of separation between an efficient cause and its effects began with the assumption that a moving object possesses an inherent power (*virtus inhaerens*) of its own, which renders a renewed input of power unnecessary. Motion thereby became less dependent on a *continuous* divine causality than was originally thought. Still, the real problems with the concept of causality as applied to creation began with the founders of mechanistic physics.

Descartes and Newton considered God's creative act indispensable for bringing the physical mechanism into being as well as for setting it in motion. Such a dependence on God obviously surpassed what Pascal unfairly described as "a mere flip of the hand" to start motion. Descartes never restricted God's creative impact to a single communication of divine power: for him, creation included a never-ending act of preservation, without which the cosmos would immediately return to nothingness. In the third *Meditation* he writes: "The same power and action are needed to preserve anything at each individual moment of its duration as would be required to create that thing anew if it were not in existence. Hence the distinction between preservation and creation is only a conceptual one."[8]

Nonetheless, the only notion of causality operative in the new cosmology was the so-called efficient one. Soon philosophy followed suit and with rare exceptions (Leibniz was one of them) reduced all forms of causality to one conceived on the model of the mechanistic theory of motion. Creation had always been interpreted in a causal way, but never as the exclusive effect of an efficient cause: God was as much formal as efficient cause.

Before continuing this search we must pause and wonder: Was it really the sciences that bear the main responsibility for the origin of modern atheism ? Or was it what religion did with the sciences, as Michael Buckley argues? After all, to the great pioneers of the physical sciences, Galileo, Kepler, and Newton, religion and science had appeared more than compatible. For Galileo, the Bible and physics merely spoke a different language. Kepler went even further and declared science a religious complement to Scripture. The latter is the tongue of God, the former the finger of God. According to Newton, science supports religion, by establishing a "fundamental religion" as ground for the divine revelation of Scripture.

The real problem, according to Buckley, was that religion came to rely on scientific conclusions, thereby indicating that it possessed no resources of its own to defend itself. It thereby traded in all that was specific and personal in the religious experience for the imper-

---

8. René Descartes, *Meditations*, in *The Philosophical Writings of Descartes,* trans. John Cottingham et al. (Cambridge: Cambridge University Press, 1984), vol. 2, p. 33.

sonal conclusions of modern cosmology. "To bracket the specifically religious in order to defend the God of religion was to assert implicitly the cognitive emptiness of the very reality one was attempting to support."[9] Acknowledging its presumed inadequacy for grounding itself, religion turned to scientific evidence for establishing its own reasonableness. But in doing so it accepted an impersonal construction that in no way corresponded to the living, personal presence of faith. Dialectically, "the denial of God was generated by the very strategies that were constructed to combat it" (p. 38).

This thesis sheds welcome new light upon the drama of modern atheism. Still, we may wonder whether the turn to scientific conclusions was not a necessary, albeit an insufficient, move, once science had opened a new area of knowledge that appeared to make the traditional interpretations of creation inadequate. For theology to ignore the new discoveries of science would have been disastrous for the rational justification of faith. Religion needed the assistance of science for proving that the new cosmology had not destroyed the reasonableness of religion. It does so today—think of the work of theologians such as Pierre Teilhard de Chardin, A. R. Peacocke, Ernan McMullin, or Michael Buckley himself. The mistake of early modern theologians consisted in taking scientific theories as if they provided basic interpretations of the meaning of religion. They should have stated, as Buckley suggests, that God is *given* in his effects rather than simply inferred *from* his effects (p. 68).

For Buckley, the heart's implicit desire for God weighs heavier than scientific arguments. The inner argument of the actual religious experience precedes any discussion of objective philosophical theories. Such was the case with Thomas Aquinas and with later theologians such as Malebranche and Pascal. He is undoubtedly right. But theologians also needed to confront the new cosmology and show its compatibility with traditional faith. How necessary this was

---

9. Michael J. Buckley, S.J., *Denying and Disclosing God: The Ambiguous Progress of Modern Atheism* (New Haven: Yale University Press, 2004), p. 37.

appears in the eighteenth-century discussion of motion, as initiated by Diderot.

Modern physics neither required nor permitted special divine intervention. Once it was in motion, the mechanistic system ruled itself. Even the *start* of motion ceased to be the crucial problem it once had been, after Newton's principle of inertia had abrogated the traditional assumption that rest had a natural priority over motion. If we also abandon, then, the unproved principle that the cosmos must have a beginning, the need for an efficient cause of motion beyond the universe ceases to exist. Such was the conclusion of Diderot and of all later French materialists.

Diderot attempted to solve the additional problem of how life could emerge from inorganic matter by assuming that matter possessed creative powers, which far exceeded the ones needed to maintain mechanical motion. Diderot claimed to see them at work in the generative process: life originates from the union of sperm and ovum, neither one of which, he thought, was a living being. Could life itself, then, not result from matter's internal evolution? Does life, even mental life, become more intelligible by ascribing its origin to an unknown cause beyond nature rather than to nature's own development? The dynamic conception of matter has resurfaced in contemporary naturalism's explanation of mental life through the drive toward self-preservation obvious in all life and, by analogy, presumed to be present also in matter.

Was this scenario less probable than that of God creating a chaos from which a universe worthy of God's wisdom and power was never to emerge, Diderot asked? Moreover, the presence of some order in the universe, though not enough to prove it to be the work of a perfect Creator, could be explained by the fact that disorder eliminates itself. In his *Letter on the Blind,* Diderot attributes to the blind Oxford mathematician Saunderson his own theory of evolutionary improvement. He describes the dying Saunderson as defending the spontaneous origin of order out of chaos: "I conjecture that in the beginning, when fermenting matter was hatching out the universe, blind men such as myself were quite common. And why should I not assert what I believe about animals to be true of worlds also? How many maimed and botched worlds have melted away, reformed themselves, and are perhaps dispersing again at any given moment, far away in space?"[10] Why could order not have originated through a natural elimination of forms incapable of being assimilated within the whole?

The *Letter* caused a scandal, especially when it became known that Diderot had placed a fictional account into the mouth of a famous scientist, who had died as a devout Christian. In his three *Dialogues with d'Alembert,* Diderot advanced his hypothesis a step further. If motion might have been inherent in nature from the beginning and if matter be conceived as dynamic rather than inert, indeed, most likely endowed with a universal sensitivity, then over a long period of time nature could have arranged itself into an orderly cosmos, and possibly have been capable of producing intelligent life. D'Holbach, La Mettrie, and Helvétius took it upon themselves to draw the conclusions, and materialist atheism was born.

Freedom and Causality

The reduction of causality to efficiency and of creation to efficient causality led to even greater problems in the moral area. Morality had remained deism's chief defense against naturalist assaults. Indeed, deists had virtually identified the content of religion with the sanction of moral rules. But the conflict between freedom and necessity, which had already been severe during the sixteenth- and the early-seventeenth-century disputes on divine predestination, intensified as the implications of an idea of creation conceived exclusively in terms of efficient causality became fully evident. Freedom as a self-constituting spontaneity is indeed incompatible with dependence on a causal agency outside itself. True freedom cannot be but autonomous. Kant had therefore excluded any divine interference from the moral act. The moral imperative originates in human conscience as the voice of reason.

---

10. Denis Diderot, *Lettre sur les aveugles,* in *Oeuvres,* ed. Laurent Versini (Paris: Robert Laffont, 1994), vol. 7, p. 167; trans. Derek Coltman in *Diderot's Selected Writings* (New York: Macmillan, 1966), p. 23.

Nietzsche's atheism originated in the conflict between God conceived as the absolute source of value on one side, and freedom that must establish its own values, on the other. At the same time the German thinker realized that without an absolute foundation, freedom becomes caught in an unlimited competition of relative and potentially self-destructive choices. For that reason he regarded the death of God as *the* symbolic event of the age. "The greatest recent event—that 'God is dead', that the belief in the Christian God has ceased to be believable—is even now beginning to cast its first shadows over Europe. For the few, at least, whose eyes, whose suspicion in their eyes is strong and sensitive enough for this spectacle, some sun seems to have set just now and some ancient and profound trust has been turned into doubt. . . ."[11] The term *God,* as Heidegger has shown, refers in this context not only to the Christian God, but to the entire suprasensory realm of ideals, including such secular ones as progress, science, and reason, which modern times have substituted for God.[12] That the entire realm of values is devalued, according to Nietzsche, is the essence of nihilism. Therefore, Heidegger concludes, nihilism is the fundamental event of Western history. It has inescapably led that history to "atheism."

The notion of a divine Creator conceived exclusively as an efficient cause conflicted with the modern idea of history as the outcome of free actions, an idea which inspired such eighteenth-century historians as Montesquieu, Voltaire, and Gibbon. Moreover, the idea of a divine Providence guiding humanity along a predetermined course would bar the road to progress. Religion had traditionally supported the social status quo as being divinely preordained.

The concept of a divine meaning in history added still another problem. How could values have been divinely established from all

---

11. Friedrich Nietzsche, *The Gay Science,* Book V (1887), #343, trans. Walter Kaufmann, in *The Portable Nietzsche* (New York: Viking Press, 1954), p. 447.

12. Martin Heidegger, "The Word of Nietzsche: God Is Dead," in *The Question Concerning Technology and other Essays,* trans. William Lovitt (New York: Harper and Row, 1977), pp. 64–66.

eternity, when they varied so much from one time to another? How could the eternal truth of religion, which Christianity claimed to possess, be contained in one historical faith? What, then, would be the fate of humans or other intelligent beings living at different times or in different places, not to mention other planets, if Fontenelle's and Diderot's hypotheses of the plurality of worlds proved to be true? What used to be a strong argument in support of Western monotheism, namely, its universal acceptance by the most advanced civilization, turned out to be its Achilles' heel, once the boundaries of the known world came to be extended. From a global perspective, former absolutes turned out to be narrowly European assumptions. How could a divine source of morality have resulted in such a multitude of contradictory values? Moreover, as Lessing had questioned, how could historical evidence ever establish universal truth? Yet all Western religions *are* historical.[13]

If the idea of freedom is incompatible with creation conceived in terms of efficient causality, we may nevertheless wonder whether freedom itself does not include an element of transcendence. Do the limiting conditions, within which freedom operates, not indicate that its very existence is a *given,* natural fact, "opaque and gratuitous"?[14] I possess neither knowledge of, nor control over, the source of my freedom. Indeed, I am not free to be free. Its norms and ideals, even its actualization, cannot but be autonomous. Yet the contingency of its existence (its *being there*) as well as the conditionedness of its operation, indicate that it does not justify itself. Modern atheism rejects any transcendent dependence, because it conceives such a dependence to be the effect of efficient causality. Yet the older concept of causality also includes other modes of dependence. Within the Neoplatonic tradition, participation in a transcendent source

---

13. Lessing, "On the Proof of Spirit and Power," in *Lessing's Theological Writings,* trans. Chadwick, p. 53.

14. Henry Duméry, *Foi et interrogation* (Paris: Téqui, 1953), p. 100; trans. Stephen McNierney and M. B. Murphy in *Faith and Reflection,* ed. Louis Dupré (New York: Herder and Herder, 1968), p. 17.

would make freedom dependent in its existence without predetermining its operation.

Its resistance to any form of transcendent dependence has induced modern atheism to reduce religion to a subjective projection. Anticipated in Hume's *Natural History of Religion,* the projective theory was first fully articulated by Feuerbach. Indeed, the English term *projection* seems to have been applied to religion by George Eliot in her translation of Feuerbach's *The Essence of Christianity.* In that work he argues that humans project upon gods the perfection of those qualities which they find only imperfectly present in themselves. The young Marx gave a social twist to the theory by interpreting religion as a utopian projection needed to compensate for unsatisfactory social conditions.

In Freud's writings, religion appears as a more complex phenomenon. He attributed its origin partly to an attempt to cope with the guilt incurred in the child's oedipal relation to the father and partly to a human desire to regain the original wholeness with nature. Projection does indeed play a role in building the phenomenal content of the religious act. But this fact does not answer the metaphysical question: Is the apparent givenness of human existence the result of a transcendent dependence, or is the nature of the human subject such that it intrinsically excludes such a transcendence? Instead of arguing that question, projectionist theories mostly dismiss it as being itself projectionist. Most atheist theories presuppose a monist concept of reality. The rejection of any kind of transcendent *otherness* is a common feature of all contemporary forms of atheism.

A secret dialectic continues to link these secular ideologies to their religious counterparts. This was particularly the case in the older (pre-1940) forms of atheism, which attempted to fill the cultural vacuum left by the departure of religion. Thus Feuerbach claimed that secular humanism fulfills what, in his view, is the primary function of religion, namely, to introduce a comprehensive love for all mankind, to integrate all human values, and to set up an ideal that surpasses all finite aspirations. This conception gave rise to a number of secular "quasi-religions." Not only do they function as religions, but, according to Paul Tillich, they also appear to play a mediating role in the contemporary dialogue among the religions themselves.[15]

They stimulate their followers to dedicate themselves to causes that surpass individual interests and that integrate their lives in a manner similar to religion.[16]

Most successful in this respect has been secular humanism. One articulate interpreter describes it as follows: "Whatever it be called, Humanism is the viewpoint that men have but one life to lead and should make the most of it in terms of creative work and happiness; that human happiness is its own justification and requires no sanction or support from supernatural sources; that in any case the supernatural, usually conceived of in the form of heavenly gods or immortal heavens, does not exist; and that human beings, using their own intelligence and cooperating liberally with one another, can build an enduring citadel of peace and beauty upon this earth."[17] The similarity of this humanist worldview with religion has impressed some humanists sufficiently to call their own movement "religious."

Another secular alternative that has attracted many of our more educated contemporaries is the aesthetic one. Aside from uniting the various and often discrepant appearances of reality within a single, coherent field of vision, the aesthetic experience conveys a glow of transcendence to ordinary reality. To be sure, the concept of aesthetic transcendence, contrary to the religious one, is based on an occasional, or at least an essentially transient, experience. Most critics abstain from making ontological claims for it. Still, its intrinsically

---

15. Paul Tillich, *Christianity and the Encounter of the World Religions* (New York: Columbia University Press, 1963), p. 5.

16. The problem has recently been taken up by Michael J. Buckley in *At The Origins of Modern Atheism* (New Haven: Yale University Press, 1987), ch. 6; John E. Smith, *Quasi-Religions: Humanism, Marxism, and Nationalism* (New York: St. Martin's Press, 1994); and Louis Dupré, "The Dialectic of Faith and Atheism in the Eighteenth Century," in *Finding God in All Things: Essays in Honor of Michael J. Buckley, S.J.*, ed. Michael J. Himes and Stephen J. Pope (New York: Crossroad, 1996), pp. 38–52.

17. Corliss Lamont, *The Philosophy of Humanism* (1949) (New York: The Philosophical Library, 1957), p. 11.

symbolic quality undoubtedly adds a surplus of meaning that, without referring to an absolute transcendence, nevertheless opens a different dimension in the real. Beauty, albeit only for a moment, *justifies* the world.[18] "After one has abandoned a belief in God," Wallace Stevens claims, "poetry is that essence which takes its place as life's redemption."[19] Such an interpretation presupposes, of course, a fundamental change in perspective. Whereas previously beauty had been viewed as a reflection of divine transcendence or as an artistic imitation of a sacred model, the self-expressive or formal character it has assumed in modern aesthetics has a more ambiguous significance: it might easily develop into a substitute for religion.

---

18. Friedrich Nietzsche, *The Birth of Tragedy*, trans. Walter Kaufmann (New York: Random House, 1967), #5, p. 52.

19. Wallace Stevens, *Opus Posthumous* (New York: A. Knopf, 1977), p. 158.

chapter F I V E

God and the Poetry of the New Age

Classicism and Romanticism in Germany

Around the turn of the nineteenth century Western Europe underwent an extraordinary cultural change. After a long period of decline during the Enlightenment and a short but violent one during the French Revolution, religion once again came to occupy the center of personal and even of public life. The French Revolution had reverberated all over the continent. The horrors that had accompanied its final years as well as the French occupation of European countries had dampened the enthusiasm which had greeted its coming. This was nowhere more the case than in Germany. Friedrich Schlegel, the leader of the budding Romantic Movement, wrote: "Nothing is more needed than a spiritual counterweight to the revolution and to the despotism of material interests through which it holds our minds. Where shall we find it? In ourselves?"[1]

Many consider Romanticism a politically reactionary movement. In fact, it owed much of its initial impetus to the very revolution it

---

1. Friedrich Schlegel, *Ideen,* Fragment 41.

came to despise. Some remained faithful to its ideals even after the revolution had failed them. Among them were Fichte and Schiller. But German Romantics had never shared the revolutionaries' hostility to established religion. In the eighteenth century, Lutheran Pietism had consistently opposed the rationalism of the Enlightenment. In Germany Pietism returned in a different guise, but without abandoning its interior quality. But the Romantic *réveil* was by no means a return to the past. It aimed at accomplishing a social as well as an *interior* reformation.

One unexpected factor had played a considerable role in fostering the inward turn of the spiritual renewal: Kant's philosophy. Having traced the entire process of knowledge to the mind's productive activity and that of morality to the personal intention, the Koenigsberg philosopher had opened an inner space of meaning. Unwittingly and unwillingly he thereby laid the foundation of a philosophical idealism, as well as of much that played a role in Romantic religion. No one went further in exploring the significance of this inner space than Kant's unacknowledged follower, Johann Gottlieb Fichte (1762–1814). In his early *Wissenschaftslehre* (1794) Fichte reduced the world to a mirror of the self and a field of the self's action. Indeed, he attempted to show that at its inner core the self coincided with the unconditioned. Fichte referred to this absolute core of the self as the *absolute* and, in his later philosophy, gave it an explicitly religious meaning. In some respect he thereby rejoined the spiritual tradition of medieval German mysticism.

Although most German Romantics had little taste for the obscure philosophical systems that were sprouting up in the wake of Kant's philosophy, they nonetheless realized that Fichte, Schelling, and Hegel had opened a new dimension in consciousness, which deserved to be explored. Their views on religion were from the beginning deeply marked by idealist thought. Through his *Biographia Litteraria* Coleridge imported a somewhat decanted version of this Romantic idealism into England. The French poets Hugo and Lamartine were to move in a similar direction.

Even though the early German Romantics shared a vaguely Christian background, their religious ideas were more comprehensive than traditional doctrine had been. Romantic religion embraced all faiths and included much that earlier generations would not have regarded as religious at all. As we shall see in the next chapter, Schelling, the leading Romantic philosopher, included in his concept of revelation the symbols and mythologies of archaic religions.

The work that inspired much of this speculation, Schleiermacher's early *Discourses on Religion* (1799), hardly mentioned Christianity. For Schleiermacher, a young Reformed pastor and friend of Friedrich Schlegel, true religion consisted in a feeling of undifferentiated oneness with nature. A French intellectual historian, Georges Gusdorf, appropriately describes this vague Romantic spirituality as "a divine presence *extra muros,* of which the center was everywhere and the circumference nowhere."[2] Unhemmed by institutional or dogmatic borders of established religion, it displayed an unprecedented openness to all faiths.

Next to this comprehensive syncretism, and often in conflict with it, the new religious movement also displayed strong eschatological tendencies. The proclamations of the French Revolution had inspired Romantics in France, but also in England and Germany, with a messianic hope for the coming of a universal brotherhood. In France this produced a half-Christian cult of *humanity* among socialist writers (Saint-Simon, Leroux, Quinet, and Sand), who were severely critical of traditional Christianity. I intend to restrict the present discussion to Germany, the country where Romantic poetry, philosophical idealism, and ecumenical theology first merged into a new identity. In the next three chapters I shall successively review the religious import of each of these movements.

Romanticism entered Germany in the form of a literary movement, magniloquently named *Sturm und Drang* after one of its more chaotic theatrical productions. It had no clear program beyond that of replacing the French domination of letters by an authentically German literature and of granting to emotion and feeling a priority over reason and morality. The new ideal was first formulated by

---

2. Georges Gusdorf, *Du néant à Dieu dans le savoir romantique* (Paris: Payot, 1983), p. 287.

Johann Gottfried Herder. According to this seminal thinker, a culture thrives only in its native soil, and there alone does it develop organically. Only by following its own immanent teleology is it capable of contributing to the building of a comprehensive human culture. Both Goethe and Schiller stood at the origin of the movement but soon took their distance from it.

Nor did they follow their younger contemporaries, Schlegel, Schleiermacher, and Novalis, into the Romantic Movement proper. Inspired by the excavations of Pompei, by Winckelmann's writings on Greek art, and by the powerful revival of ancient philology at a few German universities, Goethe and Schiller introduced a new classical literature. Yet their classicism had little in common with the sedate appeal to Greek and Latin authorities by which figures of the Enlightenment attempted to show the permanent quality of their own concepts of truth and morality. The new classicists, no less than the Romantics, were intent on changing the nature of man.

I have selected three poets whose work acutely reflects the tension accompanying the advent of the new age: Goethe, the genius in all forms of poetic expression; Schiller, the leading dramatist of the period; and Hölderlin, whose lyrical poetry, written in the first years of the century, remained unsurpassed during the rest of it. All three were deeply concerned with the religion of the future, though much in their religious views continued to reflect conceptions of the Enlightenment.

Goethe: The Promethean Mind

Through his mother's friend Susanna Katharina von Klettenberg, the young Goethe had become acquainted with the religion of the pietistic Moravian Brethren. By the time he wrote his early *The Sufferings of Young Werther (Die Leiden des jungen Werther)* (1774), he had severed all ties with traditional Christianity, though much in that novel still reflects the religion of the heart, which had inspired his earlier days. Moreover, the piety of the "beautiful soul" is movingly, though not without a touch of irony, recalled in the sixth book of

Wilhelm Meister's Apprentice Years. Nonetheless, in that same year (1774) he wrote his poem "Prometheus," in which the notorious verses appear:

Cover your heaven, Zeus, with smoke of clouds—

. . . .

I know nothing poorer under the sun than you gods—

. . . .

Should I adore you? Why? Have you ever softened the pain of sadness?

What did the writer of "Prometheus" have in mind? In the first place, that humanity was, at last, taking full possession of what was its own. Kant had described the Enlightenment as "man's release from his self-incurred tutelage." For him, as for most thinkers of the Enlightenment, it had meant that humans henceforth would no longer be subject to any other authority but that of reason. Goethe gave the idea a pantheistic twist. In his poem he expected humanity to regain its God-consciousness, which it had surrendered to the gods. In an unfinished drama of the same name and written around the same time, Goethe presents the mythic hero, symbol of the rebellious poet, as possessed by the goddess Minerva.

"A Godhead spoke when I thought I was speaking
And when I thought that a Godhead spoke, I spoke.
And with you and me so united, so intimate,
For ever my love to you."
(Act I, vv. 100–116)

In the end, Zeus no less than Prometheus stands under the rule of Fate. Zeus merely controls the order of succession, through which Fate unfolds destiny. Goethe's mythical language does not reveal whether the poet continued to admit some mode of transcendence beyond a divine immanence in nature,.

Goethe admired the beauty and moral depth of Christianity. He never stopped referring to it in his works. He also had a lifelong interest in its relation to other religions, as appears in the short treatises he added to his late collection of poems, *West-östlicher Divan*. But his Promethean ideal of *Selbstbildung* excluded any submission to rite or dogma. During his visit to Rome he attended a liturgical service in St. Peter's Basilica and wrote: "Nothing made what people call an impact on me or really impressed me, though I admired everything."

The full complexity of Goethe's religious attitude appears in *Faust,* the play on which he worked from his early years until the end of his long life. In 1790 he published a "fragment" that contains much of the dramatic plot of *Faust I,* the full text of which appeared in 1808. *Faust II* appeared posthumously in 1832. The origins of the story are well known: in a sixteenth-century chapbook Faust turns up as a magician who had sold his soul to the devil. In the next two centuries the subject of this story continued to lead a humble existence in German puppet theatres. Goethe's drama presents Faust as a scholar of many disciplines, already well-versed in magic. In the thralls of a midlife crisis he experiences the poverty of his actionless intellectual life. He knows everything but has missed the truth of life.

Faust here personifies the ambitions and frustrations of the modern person, who, inquisitive and immensely creative, feels unable to cope with the problems his autonomous self-rule have caused. He accepts nothing as *given;* all must be tried. Yet he remains aware that mysterious powers escape his grasp. He wants to control them and turns to magic. He calls up the Earth Spirit, hoping that the divine force, which makes all things live and grow, will force life to obey his will. The spirit refuses to communicate with Faust, who is obviously too immature for dealing with the powers of the nether world.

In the traditional story, Faust makes a contract with the devil to sell his soul in exchange for providing him with all pleasures he can dream of. But concepts such as "devil" and "soul" hold little meaning for the secular modern mind. Nor could the devil offer Faust what he possessed in himself. Goethe's Mephistopheles incarnates Faust's lower inclinations but also his critical self-consciousness. So he concludes no real contract with the devil. But with the help of Mephistopheles, Faust resolves to commit himself to a lifelong pursuit of experience, without ever becoming permanently attached to the object of his experience. If he does, he will be lost. Hence he must never speak the words: "Verweile doch, du bist so schön." Mephistopheles agrees to provide an abundance of occasions on which Faust may practice his resolve.

In an insightful analysis of Goethe's tragedy, Nicholas Boyle points out that Faust responds to a wager, a wager against God or any power that might seek to give meaning to his experience other than that it is his own.[3] Such a wager, Boyle adds, is self-defeating, for total self-centeredness deprives acting of its intentional, other-directed quality, which forms an essential part of the act. Since the wager confirms Faust in his destructive attitude, the play is truly what Goethe named it: a tragedy.

Twice an opportunity occurs for Faust to accept life as *given,* rather than as a self-directed project. First, in the love of innocent Gretchen. Faust is tempted to marry her. But in so doing he would lose his wager. He renders Gretchen pregnant, yet refuses to marry her. In despair she murders the child born out of their union and is condemned to be executed. Faust, remorseful of his selfishness, realizes that life is a duty imposed on us: *Dasein ist Pflicht.* But it is too late to save Gretchen. According to Nicholas Boyle, Faust is given another chance when, in the second part of the play, he gives his hand to Helen of Troy, the spirit of Greek beauty. But again he abandons her to move on to further projects. Faust's most damning act occurs at the end of the play, when he throws himself into a ruthless engineering project, without regard for the condition of the land or the people who inhabit it. In fact, Goethe himself may have signaled his protest against Faust's enterprise in the person of the "Wanderer," who visits Philemon and Baucis and dies while resisting Faust's inhumane act.

Obviously Goethe is critical of his hero and perceives the problems inherent in the modern self-asserting attitude. Yet his writings give no indication that he saw any alternative. We cannot give up an attitude on which modern life is built. Instead, Goethe attempts to

---

3. Nicholas Boyle, *Sacred and Secular Scriptures* (Notre Dame, Ind.: University of Notre Dame Press, 2006).

incorporate the spiritual riches of religion within the modern world-view. Faust, who first had called up the Earth Spirit to serve his own purposes, later prays to that Spirit with reverence and gratitude:

> "You gave me, lofty spirit, gave me all
> I pleaded for. Not vainly did you turn
> Your countenance to me amid the fire.
> You gave me splendored Nature for my kingdom,
> And strength to feel her, relish her."
>   (vv. 3217–21) (Trans. Walter Arndt)

This invocation seems to suggest some nostalgia for religious submission. So does the description of Easter morning, in which the joy of the faithful prevents the despondent Faust from committing suicide. But the passage that best represents Goethe's religious ambiguity appears in the double narrative of Faust's death. In the first one, Mephistopheles, standing before Faust's dead body, expresses his right to the soul, yet fears that it may escape him at the last moment. He cynically concludes that all Faust's dreams and endeavors have come to nothing, and his life has become a failure. In the final scene of the play, however, Faust is saved, not by his works but by Gretchen's intercession. Which ending is true? Goethe leaves it to the reader to decide.

Asked about the seemingly inappropriate happy ending, Goethe responded: "In old age we all become mystics." Yet the aging poet's borrowing of the characters of Dante's *Paradiso* does not remove the ambiguity. The final line sung by the "mystical" chorus—"Alles Vergängliche ist nur ein Gleichnis" (All that perishes is no more than an image)—indeed expresses a religious view of reality, but one that strongly deviates from the Faustian attitude.[4] Nietzsche, realizing how deep the chasm between the modern mind and divine transcendence had become, inverted the terms: "Das Unvergängliche ist nur dein Gleichnis" (The imperishable is only an image of yourself).

---

4. Cf. Klaus Hammacher's essay "Umkehrung des Symbols," in *Neoplatonismo e religione,* Archivio di Filosofia 51 (Padova: CEDAM, 1983), pp. 333–50.

Is the final scene, then, in which those words appear, no more than an ironic reference to the final canto of Dante's *Paradiso*? I think not, because Goethe conceived of the relation between God and world not like Nietzsche but like Spinoza, for whom the finite partakes of the infinite. Priority here appears to go to the infinite, as it does in Dante's religion, but with the crucial difference that the finite, more than being a mere image (*Gleichnis*) of the infinite, *is* the infinite in its finite appearance.

Even more puzzling is the final verse of the tragedy: "Das Ewig-Weibliche zieht uns hinan" (The eternal-feminine attracts us). The love of Gretchen, which follows Faust to his death, even as Beatrice followed Dante into Paradise, secures him an unearned salvation. Goethe here incarnates the Christian mystery of redemptive love in the nature of woman, who is able to love even after rejection and injustice. That love is indeed redemptive in this world. Will it also be effective in the transition to another life? That question the poet neither poses nor answers.

Yet a different view of religion appears in the later sequel to *Wilhelm Meisters Lehrjahre*, entitled *Wilhelm Meisters Wanderjahre* (*Wilhelm Meister's Travels*) (1821). Here the spokesman of the mysterious institution to which Wilhelm entrusts his son states the school's view of religion. It consists in *reverence*, in the first place for what is above us: the universal content of the religious cult. But also reverence for what is in us: religion as internalized by philosophy. And finally, reverence even for what is below us, as taught by Christian faith in the form of compassion for the humble, the poor, and the sinful. Paradoxically, this "lowest" religion is the highest one, for it alone fully accepts the earth as our dwelling place—a place of humiliation, suffering, and death. According to the teacher, therefore, Christianity surpasses and includes the other forms of reverence.[5]

---

5. On the ambiguous use of religious themes in Goethe's work, one may consult Cyrus Hamlin's excellent survey in *Religion in Geschichte und Gegenwart*, 4th ed. (Tübingen: Mohr Siebeck, 2003), s.v. "Goethe," pp. 1063–70; also, the detailed "Interpretive Notes" in the Norton critical edition of *Faust*, ed. Cyrus Hamlin (New York: Norton, 2001), pp. 345–491.

Although Goethe here, as elsewhere, praises the Christian faith, he never had any use for its dogmas. What impressed him was its moral code. Poetically, Goethe anticipated much of the modern, secular view of religion. After the scientific revolution abolished the notion of a supralunar universe, in which different laws apply, metaphysicians began to speak of one reality that had two dimensions—an infinite and a finite one. In Goethe's thought the two dimensions are so tightly united in one reality as to leave no room for *absolute* transcendence. The symbols by which he conveys this idea are transpositions of Christian originals, such as Faust's new version of the Gospel line "In the beginning was the Word," changed to "In the beginning was the Deed." Despite an abundance of religious expressions, we must take Goethe at his word: "Who possesses art and science needs no religion."

Schiller: Religion in Secular Drama

At first sight, Schiller's position on religion appears more straightforward than Goethe's. It displays none of the ambiguities, ironical poses, or intervals of piety alternating with Voltairian attacks. Schiller grew up in a pietistic family. His faith began to waver during his student years, and after reading Kant he abandoned it altogether, never to return to it. Nor did he replace Christianity by another religious worldview, such as the then popular "pantheism" of Spinoza. Despite what appears to be a clean break, Schiller's attitude turns out to be far more complex. He consistently presents Christian ideals in his dramas and even seems to preserve some notion of grace in his essays.

In his philosophical treatises *On Grace and Dignity* (*Über Anmut und Würde*) and *The Aesthetic Education of Mankind* (*Die ästhetische Erziehung der Menschheit*), Schiller describes social and aesthetic graciousness (*Anmut*) as essential to a fully moral life. Grace harmonizes sensuousness with reason and life with form. Similar to, and probably derived from the Christian idea of unmerited grace, this moral quality cannot be acquired by will power (*The Aesthetic Education,* ch. XV, sect. 4). Schiller gives a naturalist interpretation of its origin. The biological source of gracious conduct lies in the play instinct. Yet beyond this explanation we sense the presence of an idea that far surpasses the range of animal behavior.

Dignity, the counterpart of grace in *On Grace and Dignity,* likewise displays a religious connotation. Like grace, it is a human quality which, through the body, reveals the moral quality of the person. Both grace and dignity express the beauty of the soul. Schiller's description of the "beautiful soul" is free of the irony with which Goethe presents it. It refers to the quality of the naturally moral person who, without any effort to be good, merely follows the virtuous bent of his nature. We recognize the pietistic pedigree of this attitude.

Yet above this Christian foundation stands the pagan construction of Schiller's classicism. He deplores the departure of the Greek gods and regrets the coming of a stern monotheism. His ancient gods, rather than being religious models, are symbols of an aesthetic morality. In a famous poem, "Die Götter Griechenlands," he compares the Greek gods to the Christian God:

> All those blossoms have fallen
> Under the freezing wind from the North,
> To enrich *One* above all others
> This world of gods had to perish.

> (Alle jene Blüten sind gefallen
> Von des Nordes schauerlichen Wehn,
> Einen zu bereichern unter allen
> Muszte diese Götterwelt vergehn.)

With other Romantic poets, Schiller regrets the impoverishment of the aesthetic imagination deprived of Greek mythology. This aesthetic view of Hellenic mythology finds, of course, little support in historical reality.

Nonetheless, Schiller displays a genuinely religious (though not necessarily Christian) sensitivity in his dramatic works. The tragedies picture human existence as it attempts to cope with a superhuman fate. Hans Urs von Balthasar has called them "Einübungen in die Aneignung des Schicksals" (exercises in the appropriation of fate). Some of his heroes refuse to surrender to fate. Such a one was Karl Moor in the *Sturm und Drang* tragedy *The Robbers*. Others try to manipulate fate through magic, as Wallenstein did in the three plays that bear his name. Such rebels against destiny prepare their downfall. Some lose sight of their high destiny. Don Carlos abandoned the project of freeing the Netherlands for the love of the Queen.

A few submit to the forces of destiny. Thus, Mary Stuart, when condemned to die for a crime she had not committed, accepted death in expiation for her sins. In *Maria Stuart,* Schiller's most religious drama, the playwright glorifies the virtues of humility and repentance together with a hope of redemption. Mary most perfectly impersonates the grace the poet had praised in his essay on aesthetics and morality. *The Maiden of Orleans,* an obviously religious subject, presents its heroine as a passive instrument of grace. But precisely this passivity weakens the dramatic force of the religious struggle in Jeanne d'Arc's heart.

A religious idea also underlies Schiller's dramas of tragic failure, such as *Wallenstein* and *The Bride of Messina*. Wallenstein, the titanic general of the Thirty Years' War, views himself as divinely predestined to save the Empire and, in order to do so, contravenes the emperor's orders. Through astrology he tries to escape the punishment, which he knows will follow his act of rebellion. Although *Wallenstein* is a classical drama of *hybris,* it nonetheless points toward a Christian resolution by presenting the general's death as a divine punishment for insubordination to a legitimate authority. Even *The Bride of Messina,* a rather slavish imitation of a Greek tragedy of moral blindness, is inspired by the Christian idea of absolute evil, unknown to the Greeks. The destructive hatred between two brothers surpasses the Greek *hamartēma,* which actually implies a mistake.

Still, despite this presence of Christian elements, Schiller distanced himself from the Christian attitude. Like Goethe, he pursued an ideal of unconditioned freedom, inspired by a Romantic idea of the ancients, though perhaps unknown to the Greeks. Under the secular guise of his work, however, he, like Goethe, continued to honor Christian virtues, remembered from his pietistic upbringing. His tragedies inspire compassion for human weakness as well as feelings of kindness for the humble and destitute. If they are still read, performed, and in operatic versions listened to, it is in large part because we recognize ourselves more in them than in the Olympic distance of Goethe's tragedies.

Hölderlin: The Poetry of Religious Longing

In the introduction to this chapter I mentioned the eschatological mood typical of German writers around the time of the French Revolution. Friedrich Hölderlin, the greatest poet of the Romantic era, felt that the time of a new humanity had come. In a letter to his brother Karl he wrote: "We live in an age where everything is actively preparing a better future. These germs of enlightenment, these silent wishes and aspirations of individuals toward the formation (*Bildung*) of the human race, will expand and strengthen and bear wonderful fruits."

During his stay at the Tübingen Seminary and the first years thereafter, the young poet had been inspired by the moral ideals of brotherhood and patriotism, which Schiller, his model and early protector, had celebrated in the French Revolution. From this early period date such hymns as "To Humanity," "To Freedom," and "To Friendship." Disappointed by the Revolution's slide into terror, Hölderlin returned to the classical ideals he had shared with his Tübingen roommates, Hegel and Schelling. At the same time he realized that the world in which these ideals had originated was gone forever.

In that melancholy mood he wrote his novel *Hyperion*. Its hero, a young Greek participating in the 1770 rebellion against the Turkish occupation of his land, witnesses how the liberation movement degenerates into a riot of murder and plundering. The poet also had lost his faith in political action and now redirected his hopes toward the coming of an interior kingdom of love. But throughout he continued to feel a profound nostalgia for the ideals of ancient Greece. His romantic classicism differed from that of Wieland, Goethe, and Schiller, who admired Greek aesthetic principles but rarely longed for the revival of Greek culture. For Hölderlin, Greece was a sentimental homeland, enveloped by a vaguely pantheistic religion wherein the gods personified the unified powers of nature. At one point in the novel, Hyperion describes how, in a moment of mystical rapture, he envisioned the unity of all things in the principle "One and all" (*Hen kai pan*), made famous through Lessing's Spinozism. "Once I saw it, that *One* which my soul was seeking. That completion which we remove beyond the stars, and which we postpone to the end of time, I felt it present. I no longer wonder what it is: I have seen it and I have learned to recognize it."

While still working on *Hyperion,* Hölderlin attended Fichte's lectures at the University of Jena. Inspired by the philosopher's ideal of the hero called to raise his fellow men to a higher spiritual level, he wrote his drama *Der Tod des Empedokles.* In this tragedy the ancient Sicilian philosopher Empedocles combines moral heroism with religious pantheism. The wandering visionary had taught that the universal principle of love unifies all facets of Being. According to legend, the philosopher, considering his mission completed, had leaped into the crater of Mount Etna.

Hölderlin had long been fascinated by this figure, whose thought came so close to his own belief that love unites all forces of life. In his drama, Empedocles plays the role of a Christ-like redeemer who, having exhausted himself in the service of his fellow humans, is rejected by them and in the end is forced to sacrifice his life. The philosopher had unsuccessfully attempted to mediate between gods and men: to the former he owed uninterrupted devotion, to the latter, unqualified dedication. Charity induces him to reveal the secrets of divine wisdom. But thereby he betrays the gods. On the opposite side, humans resent the fact that often he withholds his divine gifts. In a later version of the play, of which only three scenes remain, Hölderlin presents the Greek sage as a guiltless sacrificial victim, who voluntarily dies for his people. This final version foreshadows the theme of the coming and disappearing god, which Hölderlin developed in the hymns he wrote during the final three years of his active life.

No thinker or poet has more powerfully evoked the sadness of living in a post-religious age than Hölderlin. In the great hymns, he sings of the loss of the gods, the abandonment of man, and his longing for the divine presence. Religion, the Christian no less than the ancient Greek one, had been reduced to a remembrance. Yet in its recollection we may still regain some of what we once possessed. In the mysterious elegy "Bread and Wine" (*Brot und Wein*), the poet meditates on the departure of the gods. Long had the Greeks known the divine as the *one-and-all,* as a holy presence that permeated the world. But not until they *named* the gods had the divine manifestation dawned upon them. In our own time, however, the gods have withdrawn from this world altogether.

> Friend, we have come too late. The gods still live
> But high above our heads in another world.

Little do they care whether we live or die. We are reminded of Hyperion's "Song of Fate," "*Ihr wandelt droben im Licht*":

> You wander amidst the light
>   On weightless footsteps, blessed spirits.
>   Radiant winds
>   Stir you gently,
>   As the fingers of the harpist
>   The holy strings.
>
> .   .   .   .
>
> But to us it is given
>   Never to find a resting-place:
>   Life dwindles and falters
>   For suffering humans,
>   Hurled blindly from one
>   Moment to the next,
>   Like water poured down
>   From cliff unto cliff,
>   Long years into uncertainty.
>   (Trans. Henry Weinfield)

Our souls are no longer strong enough to bear the divine presence. The gods have become silent. The poet wonders: What is the use of poetry in this dark time? (*Wozu Dichter in dürftiger Zeit?*) Still, like the priests of Dionysus, poets continue to wander from place to place reminding us of the heavenly ones, who may return when the time is ripe. In the sadness of this darkened world, once "a quiet genius appeared, comforting us from heaven." He disappeared but left us a memorial of his presence: bread, the fruit of the earth and of sunlight, wine, the godly source of joy. It might seem as if Hölderlin had collapsed Dionysus, the winegod, and Christ into one. But in the final strophe he resolves the ambiguity. Christ "the torch-bearing son of God" has descended into the shades of human misery to announce the end of the ancient world and to bring the promise of a new one. The night is not over yet, but "divine fires burn also during the night."

In the unfinished poem "The Only One" (*Der Einzige*) sadness returns, as the poet is caught between his nostalgia for the time when gods and men lived together in peaceful harmony and his desire for the One he loves but who has failed to return. "My Master and my Lord, how far you remain." The poem "Homecoming" (*Heimkunft*) repeats this complaint about God's departure. We even ignore His name. "When we bless the meal, whom should I name, and when we rest from the life of the day, tell me, whom should we thank? Should I mention the High One? A god does not like what is inappropriate." In "As on a Holiday" (*Wie wenn am Feiertage*) the poet expresses the hope of finding the name of God in the "deeds of the world," the storms of nature and the storms of history, harbingers of divine energy. Again, he counsels us to be patient and, for now, to be satisfied with "recollection" (*Erinnerung,* meaning both remembrance and internalization).

"Patmos," possibly Hölderlin's last and certainly his most profound religious meditation, begins with the Delphic verses "Near is the god and hard to grasp. But where there is danger, deliverance also grows" (*Nah ist / Und schwer zu fassen der Gott / Wo aber Gefahr ist, wächst / Das rettende auch*). The poet imagines he is carried away in rapture to Patmos, the island where, according to Christian legend, the apostle John wrote the Book of Revelation. The island possesses none of the beauty of the neighboring ones, but is hospitable to the shipwrecked and to homesick strangers, as it once was to the God-beloved visionary. He wants to stay near the cave where the sacred poet remembered the Christ whose face he had seen "during the mysteries of the winestock," before he left his friends. When they, sad and discouraged, wanted to move on and resume their ordinary lives, the Lord appeared one last time and then sent them his Spirit. Now the time of his return is past and our long night of waiting continues. Today even his name and the names of his followers are slowly fading. "The Highest himself has averted his face and nothing immortal remains, at the heavens or on the green earth." Yet Christ still lives. He has thrown his wheat on the threshing floor; much is lost on the ground, but enough remains to remember Him.

No more than Goethe or Schiller was Hölderlin Christian in the traditional sense. Yet more than them, and perhaps more than any other poet, he has justified the errances of the religious pilgrim in a post-Christian age: between remembrance and hope.

chapter S I X

Schelling and the Revival of Mythology

In the previous chapter I reported on the changes in religious attitudes as reflected in the classical literature of early German Romanticism. In the present one, I shall consider how these changes affected philosophy. The restoration of metaphysics enabled philosophy to discuss subjects which had long been banned from it, such as revealed religion, mythology, art, and poetry. Here I shall exclusively concentrate on the revaluation of mythology in philosophy and its import for religion.[1]

The decline of metaphysics had begun with French rationalism and British empiricism in the eighteenth century. Persuaded by Hume's critique of speculative ideas, Kant had closed philosophy to metaphysics altogether: the human mind is incapable of intellectual

1. Much of what I write here appears in greater detail in "The Role of Mythology in Schelling's Late Philosophy," *Journal of Religion* 87 (2007): 1–20.

intuitions and hence concepts unsupported by sensuous intuitions cannot be rationally justified. One of these concepts was the idea of God. Kant regarded it as necessary for integrating all others within a coherent unity, but he withdrew it, together with others formerly considered essential to metaphysics, from the realm of the properly knowable. The idea of God is an object of faith, not of knowledge.

Fichte objected that Kant himself had introduced an intellectual intuition in his theory of the moral imperative, calling it the sole *fact* of pure reason. Fichte broadened this moral intuition, extending it to the more general awareness that each agent has of himself as acting. On the basis of this indubitable perception of itself, the mind may attain a concept of selfhood as the unconditioned condition of knowledge, indeed, as the point where the ground of it coincides with reality. The main significance of this analysis was that it reopened the way to ontology.

Schelling's Early Philosophy of Myth

Few thinkers followed Fichte. Not even his earliest and most intelligent disciple, the young Schelling, proved willing to go the lonely road of pure introspection. He admitted that the access to metaphysics had been restored, yet attempted to remedy his mentor's one-sided subjectivism by showing that an intuition of nature must complement that of the self. Only a point where nature and self coincide can be called unconditioned or absolute. This correction shifted the issue from selfhood to Being and thereby renewed the metaphysical question proper. Under the influence of Boehme's theosophy, Schelling's metaphysical speculation eventually took a clearly religious direction.

Traditional philosophy is unable to answer the ultimate question: Why is there something rather than nothing? Yet ever since Plato, myth has assisted metaphysics in speaking about such vitally important subjects, which fall outside the reach of philosophy. The myth alone, according to Schelling, penetrates to the roots of existence. It was man's first attempt to understand his place in Being. Its significance consists not in an ability to articulate what philosophy is incapable of doing, but in suggesting more than what it actually expresses and thereby inspiring philosophy to move beyond its natural restrictions. In linking ontology to myth and revelation, the mature Schelling lowered his earlier philosophy to a negative preparation for his later "positive" philosophy. The task of this positive philosophy would consist in reflecting on what previously had been *revealed*. Without revelation, philosophy would remain frozen in an attitude of ignorant expectation. Mythology, in Schelling's view, formed part of that revelation.

The first announcement of a return to what for many centuries had been exorcized from philosophy appeared on a slip of paper handwritten by Hegel, but more likely composed by Schelling. "Until we express the ideas aesthetically, i.e. mythologically, they have no interest for people, and conversely until mythology becomes rational, the philosopher must be ashamed of it."[2] Whoever may have been the author, Schelling certainly was the one who followed up on the program outlined in it. Even in his early *System of Transcendental Idealism* (1800), the first comprehensive system of idealist philosophy, Schelling mentions that science and poetry were once united by mythology. The new philosophy, once again, requires the myth to bridge the gap between the realms of mind and nature.[3]

A year later Schelling himself, in his Jena *Lectures on the Philosophy of Art*,[4] started work on the myth. He argued that all art is in essence mythological. Only mythology succeeds in transforming finite figures into symbols of the infinite. In modern thought, however,

---

2. Translation in H. S. Harris, *Hegel's Development: Toward the Sunlight, 1770–1801* (Oxford: Clarendon Press, 1972), 511–12.

3. Friedrich Wilhelm Schelling, *System des transzendentalen Idealismus* (1800), in *Schellings Werke*, ed. Manfred Schröter (Munich: C. H. Beck and R. Oldenbourg, 1927), vol. 2; in English, *System of Transcendental Idealism (1800)*, trans. Peter Heath (Charlottesville: University of Virginia Press, 1978).

4. Schelling, *Vorlesungen über die Philosophie der Kunst*, in *Schellings Werke*, vol. 5; in English, *Philosophy of Art*, trans. Douglas W. Stott (Minneapolis: University of Minnesota Press, 1989). Henceforth cited by volume and page of *Schellings Werke*, followed by page in English translation.

the infinite no longer resides *within* the finite, as it did for the ancient Greeks. Hence we no longer possess a true mythology. If our philosophy is to regain the expressive capacity of the Greek one, it must, in some way, restore the ancient unity. *The Philosophy of Art* intends to introduce that philosophically ambitious project. Art *represents* in the *real* world what philosophy *thinks* in the *ideal* one. It converts the ideal determinations of the absolute—Schelling calls them archetypes—into real forms. The philosophy of art studies the relation between the archetypes and those real forms.

The artist, struggling with formal problems of expression, may not be aware of the ideal nature of his work. For the philosopher, however, that ideal quality constitutes a central subject of speculation. Art represents the ideal determinations of the absolute in aesthetic symbols. The ancient Greeks, aware of the ideal nature of beauty, personified their ideals in the form of beautiful gods. Individually the gods were finite, yet together they constituted a spiritual totality representing the absolute. "Only because they collectively form a world do the gods acquire an independent poetic existence" (V, 399; 41).

For Schelling, as for all Romantics, the primary quality of Greek mythology consisted in the beauty of the gods. Being beautiful they had to be limited. "Precisely the missing characteristic [their finitude] in the manifestation of the gods lends them their highest charm" (V, 392; 36). At the same time, by making them symbols of an ideal beauty, the ancients attempted to surpass this finitude. In the end, the tension caused by the distance between finite signifiers and an infinite signified was responsible for the demise of Greek mythology.

Christianity followed a different road. The idea of a divine Creator, totally transcendent with respect to nature, which entirely depended on this Creator, was from the beginning deemed unfit for religious symbolization. "The material of Christian mythology [to the extent that the term is still appropriate within Schelling's theory] was the universal intuition of the universe as history, as a world of providence" (V, 427; 59). The Christian worldview features no symbolic persons but only symbolic acts. The infinite no longer resides *within* the finite: it only touches it in such acts as the baptism of Christ and the act of his total surrender to God in death.

The Philosophy of Mythology

In his later *Lectures on the Philosophy of Mythology,*[5] Schelling at last undertook a detailed study of all mythologies known to him. While in the *Philosophy of Art* he had recognized the myth as an independent form of consciousness, irreducible to rational thought or to a prescientific interpretation of nature or history, in the *Lectures* he stressed the essentially religious nature of mythology. He considered mythical polytheism indispensable for the rise of an inclusive monotheism. By that he meant a monotheism so conceived that God's one Being incorporates all finite beings within itself. Despite the undeniable flaws of his work and the enormous progress since made in the study of mythology, no one has yet surpassed the scope and intellectual depth of the three-volume treatise on myth written during the final twenty years of Schelling's career. Schelling understood that neither mythology nor revelation could be simply juxtaposed to philosophy as totally independent sources of knowledge. The two had to be integrated or one would inevitably exclude the other.

To justify the inclusion of revelation, to which mythology formed a necessary preparation, within philosophical reflection, Schelling had to abandon the fundamental principle of idealism, that the mind produces all truth from within itself. The philosophical idea of absolute *Being* does indeed possess an intrinsic necessity, he granted. But such an ideal necessity contains neither real existence nor positive content. A philosophy built upon it could be no more than "negative." Only the Absolute itself is able to convert the idea of *what must be* into the reality of *what actually is.* Idealist philosophy, then, though indispensable for understanding the mind's relation to the Absolute, merely forms an introduction to the positive philosophy, according

5. *Einführung in die Philosophie der Mythologie,* in *Sämmtliche Werke,* ed. K. F. A. Schelling (Stuttgart and Augsburg: Cotta, 1856–59), vol. 11; *Philosophie der Mythologie,* in *Sämmtliche Werke,* vol. 12. Henceforth cited as volume and page of *Sämmtliche Werke.*

to which the Absolute communicates itself in mythology and revelation.

Schelling refers to the God of philosophy as *Being itself* (*ens ipsum*). Such a definition conveys no information about God's nature nor about God's relation to other beings. But if God is Being itself, all beings must be included in the idea of God. (What complicates Schelling's argument is that he uses the term *Being* indistinguishably for *essence* and *existence*. The reader is frequently forced to figure out from the context which one is intended.) In its nescience of the content of *Being,* philosophy cannot afford to ignore the concept of revelation as it has historically appeared in religion. The task of positive philosophy consists in critically analyzing the internal structure of mythology and the logic of revelation. The very nature of philosophy discloses the need for an intimate acquaintance with the Godhead. A reflection on mythology and revelation indicates that this need has actually been met. The purpose, then, of Schelling's philosophy of myth and revelation is not to "prove" the existence of a revealing God or the supernatural nature of the alleged "facts" of revelation, but to show their ideal structures.

Has Schelling not left the domain of philosophy altogether and entered that of theology? How could a manifestation of what it alleges to lie beyond the reach of the human mind ever become a subject of philosophy? He himself concedes: "Most people understand by philosophy a science which reason purely and simply generates out of itself. From that standpoint, it is natural enough to consider the philosophy of revelation an attempt to present the ideas of revealed religion as necessary, pure truths of reason or to reduce them to those" (XIV, 4).[6] To be sure, positive philosophy cannot be justified within the restrictions traditionally imposed on philosophical thought. But the question remains whether these restrictions are valid. Why should philosophy not investigate the "logic" of mythology and revelation, as it studies the logic of other forms of knowledge?

---

6. *Philosophie der Offenbarung,* in *Sämmtliche Werke,* vols. 13 and 14. Cited as volume and page of *Sämmtliche Werke.*

For Schelling, mythology forms part of revelation, even though it requires no supernatural intervention. Myths awaken the mind to full self-consciousness and prepare it to receive a "supernatural" revelation. Schelling's description differs considerably from the position of later scholars. To Paul Tillich, for instance, mythical thinking construes an early, total representation of reality, which eventually will break down into a variety of fields, such as science, philosophy, and religion. Rationalist philosophers commonly regard mythical thought as a defective, prescientific way of thinking, which contains no truth, but at an immature stage of mental development serves as a substitute of science. In Schelling's view, the myth prepares the way for neither science nor philosophy. It is an early but essential stage of the *religious* consciousness.

Schelling restricts his study of the mythical field to the genealogies of the gods, as recorded in civilizations of the Near and Far East. All myths follow a similar course, though not all complete the entire process. A complete cycle includes three stages. After a first stage, in which the sacred is not yet clearly differentiated from the nonsacred, follows a long period of polytheism, which prepares the way for an inclusive idea of one God. At a third stage, the idea of one god slowly emerges from a divine hierarchy. Schelling bases his analysis on the theory of the three *potencies (Potenzen)*, which dominates his entire later metaphysics. The potencies are neither palpable realities nor abstract concepts, but real and effective *(wirkliche)* powers that hold the middle ground between concrete and abstract concepts. "They are true universals, yet at the same time full realities" (XII, 115). In the *Einleitung in die Philosophie* (1830, but published only in 1989) Schelling describes them as ultimate conditions of Being. They raise such fundamental questions as: What precedes Being? What is needed for Being to be? Ordinary, negative philosophy is unable to answer or even to pose those questions. It starts with the existence of Being, as Hegel did in his *Logic*. Positive philosophy considers the answers of revelation, prepared by mythology, about the conditions of the possibility of Being.

Schelling distinguishes three such conditions or, as he names them in his metaphysics, three potencies. The first (A) is the mere subject of Being, which is no more than its sheer possibility *(das*

Seinkönnen). This expression assumes, as Fichte had done, that a transcendent *will* precedes actual Being. It presupposes that a pre-ontological drive renders Being not only possible but necessary: it is the condition which posits what must be (*das Sein-müssende*). The second (B) is unrestricted Being. If reality were an unconditioned response to the imperative of A, Being would be limitless and thereby destroy any possibility of being *this* or *that*. No differentiation, no particular reality, and no freedom could ever exist. The overwhelming Being of B would suppress the mere possibility of A altogether. For that reason Schelling calls the unrestricted second potency, *What ought not to be* (*das nicht-sein-sollende*). Hence, for concrete reality to be possible, a third condition must limit the impact of B. The third potency (C), then, consists in a capacity of reflection, an ability of the receptive subject to withdraw into itself and thereby to preserve the freedom to be *this* and not *that*. This third potency restrict B's undifferentiated power: B still remains the *ground* of differentiated reality, but ceases to obliterate it.

It is important to remember that the potencies are not moments of Being, but *conditions*. Hence the undifferentiated infinite Being of the B potency must not be equated with God's Being. Whereas God's Being is endowed with an infinite number of attributes, the second potency is merely indefinite and blind. In the philosophy of revelation (including mythology) the theory of the potencies plays a significant part. Negative philosophy (exclusive of revelation) is unable to *think* the transition from undifferentiated Being (B) to concrete, particular Being (C). It conceives of Being as of an empty infinite, which does not enable us to conceive of the finite as such.[7] Instead, a positive philosophy, receptive of mythology and revelation, conceives of God as infinite Being endowed with, yet not divided by, determinate attributes and by all finite beings. The possibility of conceiving a multiplicity within God first appears in mythology. It legitimates

---

7. Schelling, *Einleitung in die Philosophie* (1830), ed. Walter Ehrhardt (Stuttgart: Frommann-Holzboog, 1989), pp. 98–100. Cf. Peter Koslowski, *Philosophien der Offenbarung* (Paderborn: F. Schöning, 2001), pp. 603–4.

asking the most fundamental question, which positive philosophy is unable to answer: Why is there Being (as we know it, i.e., differentiated) rather than nothing?

Parmenides, the West's first metaphysician, consistently excluded the possibility of differentiated Being. To him, finitude and determination were mere illusions, forms of non-Being. To surpass this, negative philosophy requires an idea of Being that includes internal determinations. Only differentiated Being can justify the existence of particular realities. Polytheist mythology first informs the mind that the Absolute is internally determined and therefore able to express itself in a multitude of beings. Indeed, archaic thinking represents the Absolute itself as being a plurality and thus prepares the mind to conceive a richer, concrete idea of one God.

Formerly some scholars considered the most ancient forms of religion, which possess no polytheistic pantheon, to be "monotheistic," assuming that a pristine revelation had preceded polytheism. The mythological process thereby came to be seen as a corruption of a primeval monotheism. For Schelling, however, polytheism, rather than implying a decline of the religious consciousness, constitutes a necessary phase in the mind's ascent to a spiritual idea of God. The alleged primitive monotheism merely results from a primitive inability to distinguish the sacred from the nonsacred. At the ground of the modern "monotheist" interpretation of this archaic religion lies a theological misconception of God as *a* being among others. That dualism still survives in modern dogmatic theories, according to which the link between God and the finite consists in a relation of efficient causality between two beings. Such a conception conflicts with the idea, admitted by the same theologies, that God is Being (*esse ipsum*) and, as such, must in some way include all that is. The idea of God as Spirit, so strongly asserted in the Fourth Gospel, includes, according to Schelling, that God is present in the inmost nature of all beings. Polytheistic mythologies thereby serve the purpose of reintegrating the multiplicity of creation within the divine unity.

How, then, did polytheism start? Schelling refers to the original condition of culture, the unrestricted dominion of the second potency, as the reign of Uranos, whom Hesiod called the oldest of the Greek gods. Giving this undetermined religious awareness the name of a god misleadingly seems to make it part of the theogony. Yet, by Schelling's own account, the members of this primitive society were wandering nomads, strangers to themselves and to the lands through which they wandered; they recognized no gods at all.

In the next stage the religious mind reacts against the crushing weight of undifferentiated Being and starts justifying the existence of concrete beings. The struggle against total indifferentiation ends with the weakening of the oppressive second principle. The myth represents this process either by placing a second, female principle next to the oppressive male or by having him castrated. Urania is the name Herodotus, the fifth-century historian, gives to the primeval goddess. Under different names goddesses emerged all over the Near East. Some, such as Mylitta in Assyria, Astarte in Phrygia, or Cybele in Lybia ended up replacing the male god altogether.

In areas where the female victory had been less than absolute or where it was eventually overcome, a young male god or half-god entered the scene as a liberator of the oppressed. He mediated between the gods and the people. In Greek mythology this mysterious figure, Dionysus, had been at work long before he received a name and a place in the theogony. Similar gods appear in Egyptian, Persian, and Phoenician mythologies. Their behavior is almost identical. The young god first places himself in the service of the old one who, at least where he has not been replaced by divine matriarchies, retains much power. Soon the old god comes to suspect him of undermining his authority and tests his loyalty by imposing dangerous tasks upon him. Such were the works of Heracles (a similar half-god, possibly of Phoenician origin). The servant god survives his trials and, through the good works he accomplishes, wins the favor of the humans whose harsh lot he shares. Eventually he is killed, yet in some mysterious way is brought back to life. The old god is finally forced to recognize the power of the newcomer, even though he may not acknowledge his divinity.

Convinced that all myths followed a common pattern, Schelling tended to identify the various mediating gods of the Near East with the Greek Dionysus. In this syncretism he followed Herodotus, who had referred to the Egyptian Osiris and to the Phoenician Melkarth as Dionysus. Schelling, like Hölderlin, regards the suffering and dying gods, Dionysus, Melkarth, and Osiris, as prophetic figures of Christ. The intrinsic weakness of mythology is that by converting the potencies active in the mind's response to the Absolute into independent, divine substances, it actually arrests the process of religious development. Indeed, most mythologies even remain frozen in the struggle between the two first potencies. Their divinities never come beyond an unending fight.

Mazdaism, the noble religion of ancient Persia, constitutes an exception. In Schelling's view, it approached a true, inclusive monotheism. Unfortunately, relying almost entirely on Greek sources written well after its founding time and long before the substantial changes it underwent in the Sassanian kingdom, he knew little of the origins of Mazdaism and nothing of its later transformation. Zarathustra, an Iranian sage who lived almost a millennium before the present era, transformed a number of old Indo-Iranian beliefs and rituals into a simple, nobly moral religion. His doctrine has often been interpreted as a dualism in which two ultimate principles, Ormuzd the good and Ahriman the evil one, were locked in a permanent struggle. In fact, evil was to be overcome by the one, good principle. Despite the inadequacy of his sources, Schelling, much to his credit, perceived the monotheistic tendency of Zarathustra's thought. Even in its later, polytheistic version Mazdaism differs from other mythologies in that it overcomes the struggle between the older and the younger god. The young Mithra, rather than permanently fighting the old Ahura-Mazda, incorporates him.

The coming of Dionysus and his Phoenician, Egyptian, and Persian counterparts introduces the third potency, which reconciles the first with the second. The struggle between the two former principles ended in a defeat of the exclusive, second one. With the advent of the mediating god, the celestial kingdom acquires a spiritual, i.e., a complex, inclusive quality. The new gods prepare a different interpretation of the mythical process. The struggle against the dominant principle ends in a final reconciliation (XIII, 396–401). Only three religions, according to Schelling, completed the mythical cycle: the Egyptian, the Indian, and the Greek.

Egyptian mythology mostly stressed the struggle between the old god Typhon and the young Osiris. Typhon was originally the god of the desert, who with burning winds dried up the fertile land. Osiris restored fertility by inundating it with the Nile. Typhon kills the young god and disperses the members of his body. Isis, Osiris's sister (or bride), collects and reassembles them. Osiris, brought back to life, defeats Typhon and, according to one version of the myth, kills him, while Isis, who here appears as Typhon's spouse, laments his death. In another version, Osiris, now presented as Isis's spouse and brother of Typhon, commits adultery with Typhon's wife Nephtys.

Isis's changing role in these different versions illustrates the ambivalence surrounding the young god's coming: people prefer him but they still fear the old god. In the end Typhon merges with his young antagonist Osiris and the myth concludes with a general reconciliation. The loss of the fixed, substantial identity of the Egyptian gods indicates their beginning transformation into inner powers of the religious consciousness. When Typhon merges with Osiris, he reveals that he was not the aboriginal oppressive, undifferentiated substance, but a potency of Being confronting another potency and bound to unite with it in a third one. Osiris also abandons his substantial identity in order to become a symbol of spiritual unity, *the one who must be (der sein sollende)*. Typhon and Osiris, it appears at the end, were no more than opposite facets of the same reality. Their struggle was merely a means to restore the divine unity (XII, 374). Most significant is the dispersion of Osiris's limbs, which symbolizes the plurality that enters into the true (i.e., all-inclusive) idea of God. It also suggests that to fulfill their ideal function the gods must die.

Schelling also considers Vedic mythology to be "complete." Its main gods represent all three potencies. Yet, contrary to the Egyptian gods, they remain independent of each other and thereby fail to resolve the tensions that divide them. Brahma, the passionate, rash, and blind god (XII, 448), whom Schelling compares to Typhon, had become relegated to a mythical past. Few temples were dedicated to him and he received little cultic attention. Shiva, the destroyer who replaced him, never became more than a negative principle. The religious mind, dissatisfied with these negative deities, left them behind and moved on to a third, spiritual godhead Vishnu, the god of Being (*Sattwa*) and of light, who incarnates the third potency but has little to do with the other two gods of the supreme triad.

As Schelling presents it, Indian mythology developed in a direction opposite to the Egyptian and the Greek, which both preserved the intermediate stages as vital moments of the religious process. Hinduism thereby lost the foundational principles, the *ground* of the entire process (XIII, 403). Nor did its abrupt move to a spiritual unity satisfy ordinary believers, who reverted to more material gods. This overly simplistic interpretation fails to account for the very real relation which links Brahma, Shiva, and Vishnu. Vishnu's differentiated power could not exist without Shiva's destruction of Brahma's autocratic "monism." A text quoted from the *Puranas* (mostly written between the first and the tenth century AD) describes their intimate relatedness: "As light shows a difference, greater or less, according to its nearness or distance from fire, so is there a variation in the energy of Brahman [the Absolute, distinct from Brahma, the supreme god]. Brahma, Vishnu, and Shiva are his chief energies. Vishnu is the highest and most immediate of all the energies of Brahman. On him this entire universe is woven and interwoven: from him is the world and the world is in him; and he is the whole universe."[8]

But the main problem with Schelling's treatment is that mythology does not play the central role in Hinduism, especially in the later, Vedantic forms, that it plays in the other religions he discusses. Its role became even less significant in Buddhism, that other twig of the Indian tree. Did it originate in the ascetic and/or mystical trends of the Vedanta? Schelling's structural principles fail to explain its unique development. Nor do they shed light on Chinese "religion," which, by Schelling's own admission, possesses neither autochthonous myths nor gods!

Finally, Schelling turns to Greek mythology, the one that since the early *Philosophy of Art* had provided the model for his theory. He regards it as immediately preparing the transition to the "true" idea of God. Greek mythology, he notes, more than any other, displays a strong rationality. Hesiod's *history* of the gods raised theogony into

---

8. *Viṣṇu Purana,* trans. H. H. Wilson (London, 1840), reissued by R. C. Hazra (Calcutta, 1961), I, 22.

an intelligible system. The same concern for rationality appears in Herodotus, who claimed that the Greeks first gave names to the gods. Yet in spite of its ideal quality, Greek mythology never became abstract. At every stage, the Greeks recurred to images and often earthy representations for expressing the spiritual content. This balance between material form and spiritual significance gave Greek myths a natural aptitude for being turned into poetry.

The story of the Greek gods starts with Chaos, an ideal concept as well as a physical one. From Chaos Hesiod moves directly to Gaia (the Earth), the first female principle and the source of the mythical process. She bears Uranos, but also the mountains, the sea, and the Titans, among them Kronos and Rhea. In a second generation, Gaia bears the Cyclops, whom Zeus later used in his battle against the Titans. These primitive creatures populated the earth before it became civilized. The Greeks despised them, yet never forgot them. Their past remained vitally linked to the present and even to the future. Thus Kronos, the horrible ancestor who devoured his offspring, remains indispensable for understanding Dionysus, the latest of the gods. As Kronos, the blind force of undifferentiated Being, started losing his power, his reality broke down into a number of increasingly spiritual principles, which together formed a harmonious universe. "Greek mythology consists in the soft death, the true euthanasia of the real principle which, after its departure and demise, still leaves a beautiful, fascinating world of appearances in its place" (XIII, 405).

The ambiguous figure of Demeter therein occupies a central position. She stands between the real world of the past, dominated by the oppressive power of Kronos, and the ideal world of the future (XII, 631). Still, the memory of the simple age of Kronos (in Latin, Saturnus), continued to evoke nostalgia in the Greek and Roman minds. It was remembered as a golden age, a time when no border stones divided fields and when the earth was a common possession. Surprisingly, Demeter, the melancholy remembrance of the past, was also the goddess who introduced agriculture, the beginning of higher civilization. She never was a mere seasonal goddess. The Greek mysteries revolved around her. Nor was her daughter Persephone, abducted to the underworld, a mere image of the seed buried in the ground to reemerge after six months as a living plant. While distractedly seeking her daughter, Demeter is, in Schelling's view, looking for the lost god of the beginnings.

The Eleusinian mysteries enact the goddess's erring search for her daughter, her resignation to Persephone's marriage to Hades, and in the end, the birth of her son Dionysus. This god of the future concluded the mythical cycle, even though at an earlier stage Dionysus had been part of the polytheistic struggle. He even had been killed. Yet he had risen to new life and in the end was to survive all gods. His mother Demeter symbolized the transition from the dominion of the old god, the one *who should not be (der nicht sein sollte)*, to the higher potency of the new god *who ought to be (der sein sollte)* (XII, 634).

Persephone hereby plays a significant role. "The myths relating to Persephone contain the key to the entire mythology—a key provided by mythology itself. . . . The origins of mythology present in the Persephone doctrine move into the innermost depths of human existence" (XII, 181). She represents the dangerous odyssey of freedom as it begins to assert itself—with tragic consequences and painful compromises. Her life begins in a state of innocence, yet she is vaguely aware of her ability to move out of this pristine state. As she tests her independence by wandering off on her own, the god of the underworld abducts her to his kingdom of darkness. In response to the pleas of her mother, Hades agrees to let her spend half a year above ground and the other half in the underworld. Beyond the obvious seasonal reference, Schelling finds in Persephone a primeval symbol of the destiny of freedom, which moves from innocence to fall to rebirth. Consciousness has to die to its natural life in order to attain spiritual awareness.

Yet a third god plays a part in the Eleunisian mysteries: Dionysus. In Greek mythology he appears in three different impersonations. First as the chthonian Zagreus, the wild son of Zeus and Persephone, still very much a figure of the rustic, primitive age. The second Dionysus, the so-called Theban Bacchus, son of Zeus and the nymph Semele, incarnates the joy and revelry that accompanies the liberation from the old god. In his murder (similar to Osiris's) by raging maenads who tear the limbs off his body, Schelling sees a symbol of the fragmentation into many gods. It is, however, the third Dionysus, Iakchos, the son of Zeus and Demeter, who stands central in the mysteries (cf. XIII, 465–83). Iakchos assumes some features of the first and the second Dionysus. The hierophant still refers to him as Zagreus, and the suffering and death of Bacchus play a crucial part in the holy ritual. Yet, as we shall see, his significance lies elsewhere. He is the god of the future.

The mysteries form the transition from mythology to revealed religion: they disclose the esoteric meaning of the myth. Demeter, resigned to the loss of Persephone and of the old god, resolves the existential tensions represented by the struggling gods. The dramatic presentation of the mysteries forced the participants to confront the primeval terror hidden in the mythical narratives. Yet in the end the initiation promised a lasting beatitude indestructible by death. The reliving of Persephone's descent to Hades concluded in an encounter with the god of life. Hades and Dionysus are one, as Plutarch had cryptically written. While reenacting the mythical events, the mysteries liberated the mythical process from its oppressive materiality.

The initiation into the mysteries has often been compared to an introduction to philosophy. In the *Phaedrus,* Plato likens the goal of philosophy to that of the mysteries, namely, to move from the material to a spiritual realm, where death has no more power over life. Still, the mysteries contain no philosophy. They have more in common with the Greek tragedy, which was believed to have originated in songs commemorating the suffering and death of Dionysus. In Athens the performances still began with a sacrifice to the god of the mysteries. All that evoked pity and fear in the tragedy, the unpredictableness of human fate and its inevitable end, the initiates intensely experienced while participating in the trials of the suffering god.

The religious interpretation of Schelling's theory of myth has found scant approval among contemporary scholars. Indeed, for some, such as Claude Lévi-Strauss, religion has hardly anything to do with myth: it consists in symbolic models of social structures employed by the "savage mind" to justify the existing ones or to promote alternative ones. Lévi-Strauss's theory has introduced new social elements, but it has left out a part of the myth, which, with

Mircea Eliade, most scholars continue to recognize as essential to it. For Schelling the myth constitutes a necessary stage in the mind's development toward transcendence. Its specific function consists in preparing an idea of God that, rather than excluding finite beings, includes them within itself.

Schelling's decision to build a general theory of myth on the limited basis of Near Eastern and Greek mythologies, while omitting Oceanian, Germanic, and Slavic ones, is hard to defend. Yet what has been most seriously attacked from the beginning is the philosophical schema of the three potencies, with which he, without adequate empirical evidence, has burdened his interpretation. He thereby weakened the success of his intended project, namely, to explore the "internal logic" of the myth.

In his *Philosophy of Revelation* Schelling attempted to show that Christian revelation, the only kind he considered, was the ultimate goal of mythology and the fulfillment of promises implicit in the Greek mysteries. In that profound but controversial work, he applied the theory of the potencies to Christian monotheism, in order to justify the trinitarian interpretation of the idea of God. The history of polytheistic religion thereby becomes a preparatory episode in the manifestation of God's intra-trinitarian drama, the first act of humanity's return to its divine source. The potencies, which in the mythologies stood in opposition to one another, become gradually integrated in the process of revelation. The mythological process itself, however, remains essentially a natural one, which follows the often unpredictable course of human imagination. To the Christian claim that the Old Testament prepared Israel for the appearance of Christ as Messiah, Schelling adds that pagan mythology inspired the nations to wait for "the god who comes." In most mythologies he detects a longing for liberation from a blind, oppressive power. What paganism interpreted as the crushing power of an ancient god he compares to Luther's *wrath of God* in the Old Testament and to Boehme's *Unwill* in God.

To some Romantics, Christianity itself appeared to be no more than a continuation of the myth of the liberating god and Christ a new impersonation of Dionysus. But according to Schelling, a fundamental difference separates the Christian revelation from the myth:

whereas myth is entirely a product of the creative imagination, revelation follows a historical course (XIV, 229–33). Sagas and legends may have embellished its historical core. But they could do so only because of the essentially historical character of the Christian revelation. Schelling recognizes the presence of mythical elements in the Old Testament. The prophets fought an unceasing battle against the influence of the myths of the Near East. But he draws a sharp line between the Christian Gospel and the continuing presence of myth in the Hellenistic culture. He fails to explore, as Lessing had done, the critical question whether the infiltration of legend and myth could leave the message intact.

Contemporary philosophers have objected to Schelling's method. Walter Schulz, in a classic study, claims that Schelling's "positive" philosophy remained essentially idealist and as "negative" as Fichte's and Hegel's.[9] What Schelling ascribes to divine revelation had in fact been predetermined by the philosophical structure of his theory. The allegedly *real* God of revelation still remains the God of philosophy. Schelling might have replied that positive philosophy is indeed philosophy, but philosophy *mediated by faith,* and consequently that his "positive philosophy" was not essentially different from Anselm's *fides quaerens intellectum.* Yet the name of such an approach has traditionally been theology rather than philosophy. On the other side, to the extent that philosophy a priori determines the nature of the content, as it does in the application of the theory of potencies to revelation, it is indeed philosophy, although perhaps not positive philosophy, as Schelling intended. What may initially have been meant to be a method for *understanding* the content of mythology and revelation, soon turned into the content itself. Symptomatic of the domination by philosophy is the fact that Schelling unreservedly equates the Christian idea of reconciliation with the philosophical category of mediation.

---

9. *Die Vollendung des Deutschen Idealismus in der Spätphilosophie Schellings* (Pfullingen: Neske, 1975).

Despite these questions, the *Lectures on the Philosophy of Mythology* remains a great work. Typical of the Romantic mind is Schelling's receptive attitude to myth and revelation. He neither dismisses the former as false nor does he reduce the latter to a rationalist construction, as was often done during the Enlightenment. Everywhere his theory shows a new openness to a field that had been neglected during the previous two centuries as unworthy of scientific or philosophical attention.

chapter S E V E N

The Rebirth of Theology

Schleiermacher and Kierkegaard

In the preceding two chapters I have sketched a fundamental change that occurred at the beginning of the nineteenth century in the attitudes toward religion as reflected in the works of poets and philosophers. How did the theologians, who dealt professionally with the Christian religion, accommodate the more comprehensive concept of religion within the restricted boundaries of that tradition? We must remember that Enlightenment theology in Germany had already considerably enlarged some of the basic concepts of Christian doctrine, among them the interpretation of the historical narratives of Scripture, the influence earlier cultures exercised upon the Hebrew and the Christian, and, above all, the essentially developing nature of a historical religion. Even more extreme interpreters, such as Reimarus and Lessing, had pretended still to remain within the Christian tradition, while more conservative ones, Catholics, Protestant Pietists, as well as a large number of "orthodox" Lutherans, admitted no innovations.

The new religious climate presented even greater challenges. Both the rationalism of the progressives and the exclusivism of the conservatives were out of tune with the dynamic, revolutionary mentality of the Romantics. In the confused theological climate at the end of the eighteenth century, a young Prussian pastor began his influential career by simply ignoring all established presuppositions. One could hardly better describe Friedrich Schleiermacher's significance than in the words of his great biographer, Wilhelm Dilthey: he molded the scattered elements of modern culture into an original whole.[1]

Though he belonged to the earliest group of German Romantics, Schleiermacher reestablished the link of the movement with religion, which the Prometheism of the early Romantic models, the young Goethe and Schiller, had considerably weakened. Moreover, he was one of the most successful evangelists of his time. People flocked to the weekly sermons, which he preached for forty years—the last twenty-five years in Berlin's Trinity Cathedral. A formidable classicist, he translated most of Plato into German. Together with Wilhelm von Humboldt he played a major role in the founding of the University of Berlin and became the first dean of the faculty of theology. During the French occupation of the city by Napoleon's troops, Schleiermacher, like Fichte, through public addresses restored the confidence of his countrymen. He mightily contributed to the building of the confident German culture that secured it a leading role in the intellectual life of Europe in the nineteenth century. Above these achievements stands the personal attractiveness of the man, for whom friendship and goodness always counted as more important than personal reputation.

Discourses on Religion

Born on November 27, 1768, the second child of a Reformed chaplain in the Prussian army, Friedrich Ernst David was educated by the Moravian Brethren. He started theological studies at Halle as a de-

---

1. Wilhelm Dilthey, *Leben Schleiermachers,* 2d edition, ed. Hermann Mulert (Berlin: Vereinigung wissenschaftlicher Verleger, 1922), Preface.

voutly pietistic young man. Contact with Enlightenment theology shook his religious convictions, yet all his life he remained faithful to the spirit of the Brethren. During his tenure as chaplain to the public Charité Hospital in Berlin he became associated with the young Romantics and eventually shared living quarters with their leader, Friedrich Schlegel. It was during that period that he wrote the *Discourses on Religion (Reden über die Religion)* (1799). Rudolf Otto, in his introduction to a 1926 reprint of the first edition, called it "a veritable manifesto of the Romantics in its view of nature and history; its struggle against rationalist culture and the Philistinism of rationalism in the state, church, school, and society; its leaning toward fantasy, melancholy, presentiment, mysticism."

In the dedication to his friend von Brinkmann, Schleiermacher mentions that he had written his work in response to the "enormous crisis" which the eighteenth century, "an age of epochal decline," had left in its wake.[2] As the subtitle, *Speeches to Its Cultured Despisers* (*An die Gebildeten unter ihren Verächtern*) indicates, the book had a polemical edge against his contemporaries. From the beginning Schleiermacher had maintained some intellectual distance from the secular icons of the early Romantic Movement: Goethe, Schiller, the early Fichte. His critique was aimed more at them than at the theologians of the eighteenth century. Schleiermacher challenged the prejudices

---

2. Friedrich Schleiermacher, *Reden über die Religion: An die Gebildeten unter ihren Verächtern*, critical edition by G. Ch. Bernhard Pünjer (Braunschweig: Schwetschke, 1879). Pünjer clearly indicates the variations in each of the three editions of Schleiermacher's work. For passages common in the three editions as well as for those that appear only in the first edition, I refer to the readily available Philosophische Bibliothek edition (Hamburg: Felix Meiner, 1958, with recent reprints), indicated either as *Reden* (common) or as *Reden* I (with my translation). I refer to the second and third editions as *Reden* II and III, followed by the pagination in Pünjer.

In English, *On Religion: Speeches to Its Cultured Despisers*, trans. John Oman (1893) (New York: Harper and Brothers, 1958). Oman's translation is based on the third (final) edition of *Reden*. I refer to it as *Disc.*

The dedication appears in *Reden* I, p. 173.

of the new generation. "The different existing manifestations of religion you call positive religions. Under this name they have long been the object of a quite pre-eminent hate. Despite your repugnance to religion generally, you have always borne more easily with what for distinction is called natural religion" (*Reden* III, Pünjer, 243; *Disc.*, 214). In fact, the Romantics felt no more sympathy for the theology of the Enlightenment than Schleiermacher himself did. Nor did the young theologian come closer to "positive" religion than his adversaries had done. His was a new form of natural religion, one that did not constrain feeling and life, but rather heightened the awareness of them. Released from dogmatism and moralism, religion had to enable the mind to plumb the archaic layers of consciousness.

For Schleiermacher, experience constituted the core of religion. Neither God nor faith are part of this core. It emerges at that primeval moment of the awakening consciousness before it splits into subject and object, and before it distinguishes reality from its own ideal nature. In that state of *pure feeling,* consciousness has not yet become intentional. "You must apprehend a living movement, you must know how to listen to yourselves *before* your own consciousness. At least you must be able to reconstruct from your consciousness your own state. What you are to notice is the rise of your consciousness and not to reflect upon something already there" (*Reden* II and III, Pünjer, 53; *Disc.*, 41).

Only in memory can the mind recapture that moment of total unity. "It is the first contact of the universal life with an individual. It fills no time and fashions nothing palpable. It is the holy wedlock of the Universe with the incarnated Reason for a creative, productive embrace" (*Reden* II and III, Pünjer, 55; *Disc.*, 43). What is Schleiermacher attempting to express in these baroque phrases? Is religion a feeling that can be grasped only in memory? We think of Plato, who taught that all knowledge is recollection. But the identification of the absolute with "the Universe" points in the direction of Spinoza (*Reden* II and III, Pünjer, 52; *Disc.*, 40). Yet another, more important factor is the analogy of the religious with the aesthetic experience. Both are feelings and as such precede the division between subject and object characteristic of knowing and willing. Moreover, in the aesthetic experience, as in the religious one (and contrary to the cognitive or appetitive), the entire experience remains within the mind. The poet Novalis, recently deceased, had drawn attention to the closeness of the aesthetic to the religious. Schleiermacher mentions him in one breath with Spinoza. "Acknowledge that when the philosophers shall become religious and seek God like Spinoza, and the artists be pious and love Christ like Novalis, the great resurrection shall be celebrated for both worlds" (*Reden* II and III, Pünjer, 53; *Disc.*, 41).

In both religion and art, as Schleiermacher conceived of them, we nevertheless distinguish a more subjective from a more objective aspect within the undivided unity. In the first edition he calls the former "feeling" and the latter "intuition." Feeling, which aims at nothing beyond itself, is entirely non-intentional and non-objective. Still, without some inchoate objective orientation and some particular affective tonality in the self, feelings would be indistinguishable from one another. "Intuition without feeling is nothing . . . feeling without intuition is also nothing" (*Reden* I, 41). If the mind concentrates more on its own experience, *feeling* dominates the experience. If the more ecstatic attitude of contemplation prevails, *intuition* (*Anschauung*) dominates.

Still, even with this intuitive moment, religious experience consists of "feelings," not of faith. "I do not consider that I have the right to hold the conceptions and doctrines of God and immortality, as they are usually understood, to be the principal objects of religion. Only what in either is feeling and immediate consciousness belongs to religion. God and immortality, however, as they are found in those doctrines, are ideas" (*Reden* II and III, Pünjer, 122; *Disc.*, 93, slightly changed). Only in feeling do we attain a direct awareness of the divine. Ideas add nothing to it. Religion, then, is "a feeling of total oneness with nature, of being totally rooted in her" (*Reden* II, Pünjer, 93).

What distinguishes such a feeling from a pantheistic or aesthetic sense of nature? That Schleiermacher in the *Discourses* intended to avoid pantheism is certain; that he succeeded in doing so is not. The problem stems mainly from the fact that in this early work he conceived of religious feelings as non-intentional experiences. In *The Christian Faith*, his most mature work, religious acts have become clearly intentional. Much ambiguity could have been avoided, I think, if Schleiermacher had used the term *experience,* rather than *feeling.*

The most controversial expressions appear in the first edition, where statements such as the following appear: "God is not everything in religion, but one thing and the universe is more" (*Reden* I, 74). This, of course, presents the Greek idea of the cosmos, which contained gods as well as finite beings. It gives some indication of the origin of Schleiermacher's unintentional pantheism. While writing the *Discourses* he was studying Plato's dialogues, which he later translated into German. Especially the Second Discourse in the first edition sounds more Platonic than Christian.

Schleiermacher there criticizes metaphysicians and moralists who take Plato's idea of the Good out of its original context—the universe—and raise it to the status of a Creator above the universe. Religion consists in a direct experience of the universe, which, in his reading, coincides with the Good. "It [religion] will regard the Universe as it is. It is reverend attention and submission, in childlike passivity, to be stirred and filled by the Universe's immediate influences" (*Reden* I, 25; translation in appendix to *Disc.,* 277).

What were Schleiermacher's religious beliefs at the time of the *Discourses*? It seems unlikely that he ever conceived of God as independent of the world. As late as the third edition he writes: "The usual conception of God as one simple being outside of the world and behind the world is not the beginning and the end of religion. It is only one manner of expressing God, seldom entirely pure and always inadequate" (*Reden* III, Pünjer, 133; *Disc.,* 101). He appears to be favoring a Christian Platonic panentheism, according to which God included the world, while at the same time transcending it.[3] If my interpretation is correct, "the Universe" might not be a substitute for God, but God's worldly manifestation.

---

3. Robert R. Williams correctly compares Schleiermacher's position to that of Cardinal Nicholas of Cusa in *Schleiermacher the Theologian* (Philadelphia: Fortress Press, 1978), pp. 57–73.

On the idea of a personal God, Schleiermacher's thoughts are equally ambiguous. In the later editions of the *Discourses* he cautiously expresses them: "The rejection of the idea of a personal Deity does not decide against the presence of the Deity in [a person's] feelings. The ground of such a rejection might be a humble consciousness of the limitation of personal existence" (*Reden*, II and III, Pünjer, 127; *Disc.*, 97). Piety should not be identified with conceiving the Highest Being as "one that thinks as a person and wills outside the world" (*Reden*, II and III, Pünjer, 130; *Disc.*, 99).

How we conceive of God is not unimportant, however, even if religion consists in feeling. For feelings are codetermined by the culture in which a person has grown up. The religion of civilized peoples differs from that of primitives. For the latter it tends to be less differentiated than for the former. In the *Discourses* Schleiermacher describes the capacity for religion as inherent in the human psyche. "Man is born with the religious capacity as with every other. If only his sense for the profoundest depth of his own nature is not crushed out, if only all fellowship between himself and the Primal Source is not quite shut off, religion would, after its own fashion, be developed" (*Reden* III, Pünjer 153; *Disc.*, 124). Although the ability to experience religious feelings is innate, the present and past experience of the community significantly determines the quality of the individual's feelings. As the young theologian considers doctrinal differences mere *reflections* on feelings, the truth of religion is "for all men ever the same" (*Reden* III, Pünjer, 157–58; *Disc.*, 127). It consists in viewing the infinite in the finite.

The Christian Faith

The Christian Faith (*Der christliche Glaube*) (1821), Schleiermacher's famous text on Christian dogmatics, appears to be so different from the *Discourses* that the reader would never guess it to have been written by the same hand. The author continues to defend his earlier thesis that religion consists in feeling. Yet now he more carefully distinguishes religious feelings from other ones, by specifying them as *feelings of unconditioned (schlechthinnig) dependence.* (The English

translation has *absolute dependence*.) He thereby introduces three quali-
fications absent in the theory of the *Discourses*. First, a feeling of unconditioned dependence differs from a feeling of ordinary dependence;
second, the term *dependence* implies the existence of a *whence* on
which one feels dependent; third, the feeling of unconditioned dependence by no means excludes a sense of control that accompanies
our active engagement with the world. However powerful a person
may be, he remains aware of the fact that he is not responsible for his
being-there: he has not brought himself into existence. Schleiermacher
refers to this awareness as an experience of *Sichselbstnichtsogesetztha-
ben* (not to have posited oneself).

Since the consciousness of existential dependence refers to the
ground of selfhood, subjective and objective forms of awareness
merge in it. Schleiermacher's claim to have derived all essential theological doctrines from this feeling of unconditioned dependence is
not persuasive. Although such doctrines have not been derived from
ordinary cognitive acts, they nevertheless have a cognitive quality,
which cannot be obtained through non-intentional feelings. Even a
"feeling of unconditioned dependence" is not non-intentional.

Schleiermacher asserts that the *whence,* on which the self feels
unconditionally dependent, must be God. This attribution constitutes a second point of difference with the *Discourses,* where he referred to an immediate contact with the universe as the source of
religious feelings. Now he denies that the universe, that is, the totality of spatiotemporal being, or any part of it, could be the *unconditioned* source of my being. I experience myself as a part of the universe
and hence as much an agent with respect to other parts as one that is
subjected to their influence.[4] Still, Schleiermacher does not conclude
that *therefore* I depend on an "infinite Being," which transcends the
universe. He maintains what he wrote in the *Discourses*: "It obviously

---

4. *Der christliche Glaube* (2d edition), ed. Martin Redeker (Berlin: Walter de
Gruyter, 1960), § 32, 2, pp. 171–73; in English, *The Christian Faith,* trans. under direction of H. R. Mackintosh and J. S. Stewart (New York: Harper and Row, 1963),
pp. 132–33. I refer to the German title as *CG*; to the English as *CF*.

is a delusion to seek the infinite outside the finite, as its opposite. But is [such a delusion] not natural in those who know but the surface of even the finite and the sensuous?" (*Reden* III, Pünjer, 155; *Disc.*, 125, corrected).

Whether one interprets the divine source of the feeling of dependence as single or as plural, as one or as many, does not affect the nature of the feeling. In fact, however, we observe that humans, once they reach an advanced state of culture, move toward monotheistic religion. Still, *The Christian Faith* persistently denies that the idea of God precedes the feeling of dependence. According to Schleiermacher, the opposite occurs: the idea corresponding to the term God "is nothing more than the expression of the feeling of absolute dependence . . . and is quite independent of any original knowledge (properly so called)" (*CG* §4, pp. 29–30; *CF*, 17). If the "sense of the Deity" does not include any preliminary belief in, or innate idea of God, what, then, is the status of the *whence* assumed to be implied in the feeling of unconditioned dependence? The answer must be that this feeling itself depends on a power outside the mind (*CG* §14, p. 1; *CF*, 68). But we know nothing of this power as it is in itself.[5]

A third difference divides *The Christian Faith* from the *Discourses*. The feeling of absolute dependence *includes* and surpasses even those feelings that accompany active experiences. Indeed, it spurs the believer to acts of faith. This conclusion does not contradict the earlier thesis that the feeling of unconditioned dependence is an original experience, which does not depend on any preceding idea or commitment. Nor does it necessarily result in either one, though it stimulates the mind in both directions.

Religion requires that the feeling of absolute dependence be expressed. Characteristic of all Christian dogmas is that they refer to Jesus Christ as Redeemer (*CG* §17, p. 1; *CF*, 83). Filled with the highest God-consciousness, Jesus left his followers the perfect model of

---

5. Falk Wagner, "Gefühl und Gottesbewusstsein: Zum Problem des Theologischen in Schleiermachers philosophischen und theologischen Denken," in *Schleiermacher,* ed. M. M. Olivetti et al., Archivio di Filosofia 11 (Padova: CEDAM, 1984), nos. 1–3, pp. 271–97, esp. p. 290.

spiritual life, while at the same time he granted them the ability to pursue such a life. Through its symbols, confessions, and dogmas the religious community transfers Christ's impact on his disciples to later generations. The canonical narratives of Jesus' life and the liturgical ceremonies in which the Church commemorates them serve the same purpose. Dogmatic theology brings these anamnetic actions and formulations together into a coherent *system*.

But the dogmatic formulations in which a religious community articulates its common experience ought not to constrain the individual feeling. What a community defined at an earlier time may no longer correspond to the current experience of its members. Dogmas merely serve as guideposts in the development of a tradition. Believers should not consider themselves bound by each and every one of them. Indeed, a community of faith may split apart over the interpretation of the ancient syllabi, as occurred when the Christian East broke with the West, and when Protestantism separated from Roman Catholicism.

Kierkegaard's Theology of Freedom

Kierkegaard's work forms the late Romantic counterpart to Schleiermacher's early theology. Whereas the German theologian had started from the Romantic notion of feeling, the Danish thinker took freedom, the fundamental concept of idealist philosophy, as the central subject of his theology. Schleiermacher had bypassed, rather than answered, the serious problems evoked by Kant and his idealist successors. Kierkegaard confronted them head-on. The autonomous nature of Kant's concept of freedom, particularly as his idealist followers, the early Fichte and the early Schelling, had developed it, placed prohibitive restrictions upon theology. According to their philosophy, a person can attain genuine selfhood only by actualizing his freedom without any extraneous interference.

Kierkegaard followed the idealist philosophers in defining selfhood as free self-realization. In *Sickness unto Death* (1849), he describes the self as a relation that actively relates itself to itself. How, then, is religion, which consists in recognizing one's total dependence (on that he agreed with Schleiermacher), compatible with the idea of self-constituting freedom? Kierkegaard attempted to resolve the difficulty by postulating a transcendent dimension in the relation of the self to itself. I can exercise my freedom only on the basis of a created dependence, over which I have no control. A person cannot *fully* choose himself except in a recognition of his being dependent on an absolute.

The relation of the self to itself, then, contains a reference to a fundamental givenness that surpasses and conditions his power to choose. For the implicit presence of the idea of the *infinite* within each finite choice indicates that truly to choose oneself requires accepting a factor over which one has no power. Until a person accomplishes the task of choosing himself as a synthesis of the finite and the infinite, he has not yet achieved full selfhood. Whoever refuses to choose at all, remains in what Kierkegaard calls an aesthetic state. He drifts along on a succession of experiences without definitively committing himself to any. He becomes an ironical observer of his own existence. "Life is for [the ironist] a drama and what engrosses him is the ingenious unfolding of this drama. He is himself a spectator even when performing some act. He renders his ego infinite, volatizes it metaphysically and aesthetically."[6] He or she is deterred from a definitive commitment such as marriage by an awareness that the very feelings that attract him or her today may tomorrow be replaced by similar feelings for a different person.

In the first part of *Either/Or* (1843) and in the initial essay of *Stages on Life's Way* (1845), Kierkegaard portrays various types of this aesthetic attitude. They all suffer from an indeterminate unrest. This may in the end prod them to commit themselves to a permanent relationship or to a definitive choice. The individual who makes this choice thereby accepts living within the limitations of a particular task and living by preestablished moral norms.

---

6. *The Concept of Irony*, trans. Lee Capel (New York: Harper and Row, 1966), p. 300.

An ethical choice, according to Kierkegaard, always implies a religious element. Since a full choice of myself implies choosing myself as dependent, I thereby sanction my choice by a supreme authority. Only that religious element renders the ethical distinction between *good* and *evil* absolute. By the same token I am forced to recognize that I never fully live up to my moral obligation and hence that I am "guilty before God." So I actually choose myself "in repentance." At the end of *Either/Or,* an "ultimatum" is "Before God we are always in the wrong." A later work (*The Concept of Dread*) supports this controversial assertion by a reinterpretation of the dogma of original sin.

Fear and Trembling (1843) takes religion beyond the ethical realm within which Enlightenment theology had enclosed it. Religion, though essential to ethics, nonetheless interrupts the even flow of the moral life. It always introduces the exception to the universal rules of ethics. Did God not command Abraham to sacrifice his son Isaac, a clear violation of ethics? The argument taken from the Genesis story is hardly persuasive, since its intent might have been to teach the opposite, namely, that human sacrifices are henceforth forbidden in Israel. As Kierkegaard uses it, the story refers to the religious readiness to sacrifice what one holds dearest, even beyond or against the requirements of the moral law. Religiously, humans must be prepared to accept the personal losses they are bound to suffer in the course of life. Life always disappoints our expectations of what we consider our moral desert.

Kierkegaard devoted *Repetition* (1843), his smallest book and arguably his most significant one, to the thorny question of suffering. Again he weaves his tale around a biblical figure, Job, the man who has lost everything. When his friends advise him to accept his fate as a punishment for perhaps unremembered moral violations, Job, animated by "the passion of freedom," refuses. He is resigned to the loss of his children and possessions, but he refuses to admit that he *deserves* a punishment for unknown moral transgressions. Preserving one's freedom in the religious attitude demands more than being resigned to whatever suffering overcomes one.

Surprisingly, Kierkegaard argues Job's case in terms of the question whether a genuine repetition is possible in life. The ancient Danish term for repetition, *gjentagelse,* occasions this detour. In Kierkegaard's time that term was still used in the ordinary sense of "repetition." But the etymological meaning, consisting of *tage igen,* comes closer to "recapturing," and that is what the story is about. In a witty report, the author tells us that no experience can ever be "repeated." But is there not a deeper kind of repetition? Is it not possible to *recapture* one's moral freedom, after an external power has violently interrupted it? Should one simply surrender freedom to necessity, as Job's friends advised him to do, and attribute the interruption of one's life to a divine punishment? Is one not justified in rebelling against the assault on one's freedom? Kierkegaard answers all these questions affirmatively. Job declared himself both resigned to God's will and yet morally innocent. He considered God's destructive intervention in his life not a punishment but a *trial.*

Job expects the very power that crushed him to restore, if not his possessions and children, at least his potential to act freely with foreseeable consequences. The biblical text merely reports that Job's possessions were restored. But according to *Repetition,* his existence became internally transformed, and this would have been the case even if his external circumstances had remained the same. Originally Kierkegaard interpreted this restoration in a purely internal way: outwardly the transformed person neither differs nor appears to differ from his secular contemporaries, though inwardly he leads a life of "hidden interiority." Later Kierkegaard began to wonder: Is hidden interiority not a recipe for religious mediocrity? Does Christ not call his followers to the active pursuit of a higher ideal? He became suspicious of a religion never outwardly expressed in acts of piety.

In *Training in Christianity* (1850) and in *For Self-Examination* (1851), Kierkegaard attacked, at times very unfairly, the Danish Church for never professing its faith in action. Had Christ not introduced a higher ethics? When God ordered Abraham to sacrifice his son, the author of *Fear and Trembling* had called this a "suspension" of ethics. But suspension was not suppression. Indeed, ethical obligations assume a more demanding character once they become religious duties. Luther had freed Christians from the anxiety of having to "earn" their salvation, but not from the obligation of leading an exemplary Christian life. The Gospel demanded that the believer imitate Christ, even though he acquires no "merit" through it.

Religion, for Kierkegaard as well as Schleiermacher, sanctions the modern principle of subjectivity. Yet contrary to Schleiermacher's religious subjectivity, Kierkegaard's consisted not in a *feeling* of dependence, but in a transformation of freedom and in a corresponding change of oneself both inwardly and outwardly. What was the role of *faith* thereby? Certainly not to import new knowledge, but to provide access to the believer's inmost subjectivity. In *Philosophical Fragments* (1844) and in the subsequent *Concluding Unscientific Postscript* (1846), Kierkegaard sketched an outline of the dialectic of subjectivity as directed by faith. Faith, he claims, compels the mind to move to its outer limits, where it has to abandon all objective footholds and is forced to confront itself as pure subject.

For Kierkegaard, as much as for the idealists Fichte and Schelling, the essence of mind consists in subjectivity. When reflecting upon itself, the mind has no proper object, as it does in other acts of cognition. All knowledge of the self as subject thereby becomes paradoxical, as Socrates had claimed. In the content of faith, however, the mind confronts an object that is even less assimilable. The paradox increases in intensity, for the seemingly objective message of the Gospel, "The eternal has appeared in time," surpasses all objective understanding. Objectively such a paradoxical statement can evoke only the greatest uncertainty. Yet faith converts this uncertainty into total certainty by its unreserved commitment to it.

How can the mind responsibly do so? Only by force of a divine attraction. A person may surrender to this attraction or continue to doubt (Kierkegaard does not consider the possibility of a total refusal). But in neither case does his or her response depend on the presence or absence of objective arguments: they can never be decisive in this matter. "Belief and doubt are not two forms of knowledge, determinable in continuity with one another, for neither of them is a cognitive act; they are opposite passions."[7]

Kierkegaard's religious significance in modern thought consists in his reinterpretation of the idealist principle of subjectivity. For

---

7. *Philosophical Fragments,* trans. David Swenson, revised by Howard V. Hong (Princeton: Princeton University Press, 1962), p. 105.

him, the act of faith consists not in assimilating an objective content, but in subjectively confronting a message that cannot be objectively assimilated. Because of its vital significance the message drives the mind into itself, where it challenges its subjective powers of decision. For Kierkegaard, unlike the idealists, subject and object remain permanently opposed.

When Kierkegaard in the *Concluding Unscientific Postscript* describes Christianity as "essentially subjectivity," he does not mean that the message of revelation is immanent in the mind itself, as some idealists claimed, but rather the opposite, namely, that this message is so transcendent that the mind cannot absorb it. Yet freedom, the heart of subjectivity, is being able to respond in an act of acceptance or refusal to what for the understanding remains a paradox. In positively responding to the message, freedom acknowledges that it is in its very core dependent. The confrontation with the transcendent message of faith never reaches a resolution. Faith, for Kierkegaard, remains forever "a concern" about faith.

Conclusion

Religion at the End of the Modern Age

For a final assessment of the impact of modern culture upon religion we return to the very beginning, the point where the medieval synthesis of nature and grace fell apart. This, as I mentioned in the second chapter, occurred in the nominalist theology of the fifteenth and sixteenth centuries when the term *supernatural* came to refer to a separate reality and the teleology of nature became detached from that of the supernatural order. This separation led to a naturalism that contributed to the later rise of atheism.

Paradoxically, it was the new awareness of the unity of the celestial and the sublunar realms which activated the naturalism that had resulted from the theological separation of nature and grace. When Galileo showed that the same physical laws rule the entire universe, the celestial as well as the terrestrial, was the notion of the "supernatural," then, more than a leftover of the old "celestial order"? The assumption that it was not became one of the unarticulated principles of that secularism which has so profoundly affected the spiritual climate of our time. There were other factors. We have analyzed some in the chapter on atheism. The creative confidence of the individual, awakened in the early Renaissance, led to the unqualified assertion of human freedom of the nineteenth century.

Yet I doubt that any factor surpassed the negative religious impact of ideologies that sprang up in the wake of the scientific revolution. Earlier I mentioned the dominance of the theory of efficient causality, which distorted the modern understanding of creation. Jews and Christians had always conceived of creation as effected by divine causality. But after an initial period in which they represented the Creator as the "maker of the world," they had understood that creation was not the exclusive effect of an *efficient* cause. A crisis developed when the scientific revolution of the seventeenth century eclipsed the formal and the final forms of causality steadfastly supported by Aristotle and the Scholastics. The rule that teleological considerations ought to be banned from any kind of scientific investigation had proven to be useful in ridding the physical sciences from the early confusion of systematic observation with theological speculation. Extending the ban to the life sciences had been shown to be untenable even before the end of the eighteenth century. Among the leading philosophers of the Enlightenment, Leibniz alone kept arguing that divine causality is more formal than efficient. In the moral area the concept of creation as an act of efficient causality had even more disastrous consequences. It collided head-on with the modern idea of freedom, since freedom cannot be "caused" in any efficient sense.

In the meantime the rule had become a secular dogma, which led to *scientism*, the principal one among the secular ideologies of the modern age. It presumed that any belief not justified by scientific methods may be discarded as probably false. Religious believers reacted against this scientism, but frequently without clearly knowing what they ought to attack. The recent advocacy of intelligent design merely revives the old confusion between science and theological speculation. Presented as a scientific "alternative," it illegitimately interferes both with the method and the purpose of the scientific investigation of the evolution of life, proposing as an indispensable appendix what such an investigation neither needs nor can accept.

On the other side, some biologists have unqualifiedly ruled out any interpretation of intelligent life other than the biological one.

That the evolution toward such life is a mere accident may, from a biological point of view, be a legitimate conclusion. But how far does such a conclusion extend? It proves that evolution develops through mutations which are adequately explained through chemical or biological factors. The fact that those mutations occur randomly, an essential part of the theory, appears incompatible with the idea of a preselection of the order of succession. Hence no argument for the existence of a divine orderer can be made on the basis of biological conclusions.

But the scientist transgresses the limits of his field if he denies the believing mind the intellectual right on other than biological grounds to attribute a theological meaning to a process that results in such realities as mind, self-consciousness, and freedom. To declare such an attribution "unscientific" or unjustified is tantamount to denying the legitimacy of any belief in creation and divine providence. Indeed, it implies that science and religious faith are intrinsically incompatible. An atheist conclusion becomes thereby inescapable. Yet it surpasses the boundaries of science. The biological theory of evolution is designed for investigating how one form of life mutates into another, not for explaining the presence or absence of a transcendent meaning to human existence. The claim that mind is no more than the necessary outcome of a random biological process grossly oversteps the limits of science.

Obviously, the conditions necessary for the mind's possibility lie in the biological order. Consciousness depends on the formation of a human body, including that of the brain with all its neurons. Yet the mind as such cannot be simply equated with the biological conditions on which it depends. Hence nothing prevents the believer from viewing the random evolutionary process as *theologically* meaningful. Without entering the complex issue of how brain and mind are related, it suffices to state that a biological theory cannot serve as a substitute for a belief in creation, no more than such a belief can serve as a substitute or a necessary complement for a biological theory. They belong to different intellectual orders. The conception that evolution replaces creation is a typical instance of scientific dogmatism.

Another dominant ideology of our age is that the *modern* view of things is the correct one and that any conflicting view is *eo ipso* false or at least less satisfactory. This rule is assumed to be confirmed by the fact that wherever modern civilization enters, it replaces all others. Compared to the past, modern life displays such an overwhelming improvement of material living conditions that its superiority cannot be questioned. Technology has made us masters of our world and, to some extent, even of our lives. It has prolonged life beyond any previous measure, by increasing the food supply, by creating more hygienic living conditions, by inventing the means to cure once fatal diseases and deadly traumas. These successes so far exceed the disadvantages which accompany them, that few who have once experienced the modern way of life would be willing to abandon it.

And yet, considering the state of humanity in the contemporary world, who would regard those successes as unqualified signs of progress? Undoubtedly, we live better, we have become civil, more elegant in body, dress, and shelter, we are able to express ourselves more accurately and more graciously. Yet as Kant observed, this kind of progress is no indication of moral well-being. "To a degree we are, through art and science, *cultured*. We are civilized—perhaps too much for our own good—in all sorts of social graces and decorum. But to consider ourselves as having reached *morality*—for that is much lacking."[1] Our moral growth has not kept pace with the technical and scientific advances of the modern age. Yet a technology capable of achieving a previously unthinkable expansion of mental control over the physical and social world demands greater moral maturity than we possess today. Lacking this maturity to match our titanic powers, we have committed crimes, waged wars, and wrought destruction on an unparalleled scale. Instead of strengthening our moral fibre, we have gone a long way in undermining the basis of morality. Our desire to advance technically as far as possible has made us question the very principles on which morality is based. There are few moral principles left on which we are still able to agree.

The modern age has transferred the primary source of meaning and value from nature, and thus ultimately from the Creator of na-

---

1. Kant, "Idea for a Universal History," in *Gesammelte Schriften*, VII, 27.

ture, to the human mind. Any reality other than that of the mind it-self becomes thereby reduced to the status of an object. But once the constitution of "objectivity" has become the principal function of the mind, the mind itself ends up possessing no content of its own. Kant drew this conclusion when he wrote: "Beyond the logical meaning of the 'I' [as subject of all representation] we have no knowledge of the subject in itself, which as substratum supports this."[2] The self has become a mere function of its own mental acts.

Kant's followers attempted to remedy this loss of the self's content. Fichte asserted that, contrary to Kant's denial, the mind does possess an intuition of itself. The German Romantics followed Fichte. But when that insight developed into a *science* of the self in the late nineteenth and twentieth centuries, it once again moved in an objectivist, reductionist direction. Karl Mannheim summarizes the lamentable effects of a psychology conceived exclusively as a positive science. "Meaning-giving interpretations with qualitatively rich contents (as, for instance, sin, despair, loneliness, Christian love) were replaced by formalized entities of isolation, and the 'libido.' These latter sought to apply interpretive schemes derived from mechanics to the inner experience of man. The aim here was not so much to comprehend as precisely as possible the inner contentual richness of experiences as they coexist in the individual and together operate towards the achievement of a meaningful goal; the attempt was rather to exclude all distinctive elements in experience from the content in order that, wherever possible, the conception of psychic events should approximate the simple scheme of mechanics (position, motion, cause, effect)."[3] The objectivist view implied in that approach closes the mind to any kind of transcendence and confirms the secular dogma of reality as a compact, impenetrably self-enclosed entity.

Religious language must, by its very nature, be symbolic: its referent surpasses the objective universe. Objectivist language is fit only to signify things in a one-dimensional universe. It is incapable

---

2. *Critique of Pure Reason,* A 350.

3. Karl Mannheim, *Ideology and Utopia,* trans. Louis Wirth and Edward Shils (New York: Harcourt, Brace and World, n.d. [first edition 1936]), p. 17.

of referring to another level of reality, as art, poetry, and religion do. Rather than properly symbolizing, it establishes external *analogies* between objectively conceived realities. Their relation is allegorical rather than symbolic. A truly symbolic relation must be grounded in Being itself. Nothing exposes our religious impoverishment more directly than the loss of the ontological dimension of language. To overcome this, poets and mystics have removed their language as far as possible from everyday speech.

In premodern traditions, language remained closer to the ontological core which all things share and which intrinsically links them to one another. Symbols thereby participated in the very Being of what they symbolized, as they still do in great poetry. Religious symbols re-*presented* the divine reality: they actually made the divine present in images and metaphors. The ontological richness of the participatory presence of a truly symbolic system of signification appeared in the original conception of sacraments, rituals, icons, and ecclesiastical hierarchies.

The nominalism of the late Middle Ages resulted in a very different representation of the creature's relation with God. The world no longer appears as a divine expression except in the restricted sense of expressing the divine *will*. Finite reality becomes separated from its Creator. As a result, creatures have lost not only their intrinsic participation in God's Being but also their ontological communion with one another. Their relation becomes defined by divine decree. Nominalism not only has survived the secularization of modern thought, but has became radicalized in our own cybernetic culture, where symbols are reduced to arbitrary signs in an intramundane web of references, of which each point can be linked to any other point. The advantages of such a system need no proof: the entire scientific and technical functioning of contemporary society depends on it. At the same time, the modern mind's capacity for creating and understanding religious symbols has been severely weakened. Symbols have become man-made, objective signs, serviceable for making any reality part of a system without having to be part of that reality.

Recent theologians have attempted to stem the secular tide. Two of them did so by basically rethinking the relation between nature and grace, the main causes of today's secularism. Henri de Lubac undertook a historical critique of the modern separation of nature and the supernatural. Not coincidentally, he also wrote a masterly literary study on religious symbolism before the nominalist revolution. In a number of works Hans Urs von Balthasar developed a theology in which grace, rather than being added to nature as a supernatural accident, constitutes the very depth of the mystery of Being. Being is both immanent and transcendent. Grace consists in its transcendent dimension. Whenever a poet, artist, or philosopher penetrates into the mystery of existence, he or she reveals an aspect of divine grace. Not only theology but also art and poetry, even philosophy, thereby regain a mystical quality, and religion resumes its place at the heart of human reality.

No program of theological renewal can by itself achieve a religious restoration. To be effective a theological vision requires a recognition of the sacred. Is the modern mind still capable of such a recognition? Its fundamental attitude directly conflicts with the conditions necessary for it. First, some kind of moral conversion has become indispensable. The immediate question is not whether we confess a religious faith, or whether we live in conformity with certain religious norms, but whether we are of a disposition to accept any kind of theoretical or practical direction coming from a source other than the mind itself. Such a disposition demands that we be prepared to abandon the conquering, self-sufficient state of mind characteristic of late modernity. I still believe in the necessity of what I wrote at an earlier occasion: "What is needed is a conversion to an attitude in which existing is more than taking, acting more than making, meaning more than function—an attitude in which there is enough leisure for wonder and enough detachment for transcendence. What is needed most of all is an attitude in which transcendence *can be recognized again.*"[4]

---

4. Louis Dupré, *Transcendent Selfhood* (New York: Crossroad Books, 1976), p. 17.

index of names

LOUIS DUPRÉ

is T. Lawrason Riggs Professor Emeritus in Religious Studies at Yale University. He has published numerous books and articles, including *The Other Dimension* and *Transcendent Selfhood.*